A t this very moment, readers around the world are spending far too much time at work logged into *www.arcataeye.com*, engrossed in the comic capers and desultory drollery found in the *Arcata Eye's* online Police Log. To relieve the strain on Internet bandwidth and improve global worker productivity, *The Police Log II: The Nimrod Imbroglios* offers a portable compendium of early 21st Century small-town crime in a far-up Northern California town. Read and behold Arcata's criminal justice process from initial bongo incursion to inevitable Pink House excursion.

### FROM *THE POLICE LOG II: THE NIMROD IMBROGLIOS:*

**12:58 a.m.** The whereabouts of Jeanne Kirkpatrick, Stephen Hawking and Alexander Solzhenitsin at the time are unknown, but *somebody* slathered a Sunny Brae school with soda, toilet paper, ketchup and syrup.

**4:14 p.m.** The term "defrauding an innkeeper" may evoke enchanting images of adventure and romance in medieval times – mammoth mutton legs washed down with grog from a pewter chalice; furtive rolls in the hay with a country maiden; swashbuckling escapes on a hastily conscripted steed... but in this case, a Rio Deller allegedly scarfed down some deli fare and boogied from a 13th Street marketplace. She was cited, booked and released.

**5:16 p.m.**
Near Wyatt Lane, cows took some knocks
From mouth-breathers playing with rocks
They pelted the cattle
Then broke off the battle
And dragged knuckles on down the block.

**6:47 p.m.**
Four men on L Street
Stopped, whipped it out and unsheathed
Streaming shafts of gold.

Dedicated with gratitude to the men and women of the
Arcata Police Department.

Kevin thanks Ann, Ron, Kelly, Elizabeth, Lily, Sam, Betty, Emma, Terrence McNally, Rebecca S. Bender, Jennifer Savage, Helen Wilson, Thomas J. Doyle, Dave Held, Lush Newton, Bobby Wright, Fran Roth, Stina Sieg, Bruce Anderson, Monica Hadley, Jack Durham, Kevin P. Klein, David Gans, Elizabeth Fox, all in The Well, Jim Dodge, Jon Carroll, Michelle Locke, Marjie Lundstrom, Amy Stewart, Heidi Benson, Mark Siemens, Bob Holcomb, Candy Miller, Wendy Wood, Brian Sproul, Michael and Joan Brennan, Howard DeWitt, Florence Reynolds, Walt Halland, Dana Countryman, Maggie Nystrom, Lee Wakefield, Seth Porges, Peter Fimrite, Katie Whiteside, Rosemary Edmiston, the Arcata Police Department, the Arcata Volunteer Fire Department, the Historical Sites Society of Arcata, Cory Ratzlaff, Alexis Kennedy, Alexandra Stillman, Victor Schaub, Marcia and Simeon Tauber, Pete Villarreal, Emily Siegel, Steve Gordon, Lois and Robin Arkley, the Collenbergs, Don Kolshinski, John Antonioli, Larry Valadao, L. Scott Rebman, Lenny Bruce, Frank Zappa, Mike Keneally, Ian Anderson, John Lennon, Pixton DuQuesne and all the kindly readers who've offered inspiration and encouragement along the way.

Kevin L. Hoover is the editor of the *Arcata Eye*,
"America's most popular obscure small-town newspaper," and
author of *The Police Log: True Crime & More from Arcata,
California* and *The Police Log II: The Nimrod Imbroglios*.
For 12 years, at three newspapers, he has documented
errant doings in his town's streets and neighborhoods
to the delight of readers, the enjoyment of colleagues
and the disdain of journalism professors.

***Opposite page:*** **APD Ranger Bob Murphy with a passel of
Plaza bongo pilots on a fine Arcata day in 2004.**

# THE POLICE LOG II

## THE NIMROD IMBROGLIOS

Kevin L. Hoover
The Arcata Eye
2004

# THE POLICE LOG II
## THE NIMROD IMBROGLIOS
### BY KEVIN L. HOOVER

Published by
**The Arcata Eye**
P.O. Box 451
Arcata, California 95518-0451

*news@arcataeye.com*
*www.arcataeye.com*

ISBN, Print ed. 0-9747662-1-6

First printing 2004

Printed in the United States of America

**Library of Congress Cataloging-in-Publication Data**
Hoover, Kevin L.
The Police Log II: The Nimrod Imbroglios/Kevin L. Hoover. – 1st ed.
ISBN 0-9747662-1-6
1. Crime—Arcata (Calif.)
2. Crime—Humor.
3. Crime—Northern California.
4. Newspapers—Arcata (Calif.)
5. Newspapers—Sections, columns, etc.
6. Police—Records and correspondence.

Library of Congress Control Number: 2004097464

# TORRID
# TABLE OF CONTENTS

ILLUSTRATIONS BY THOMAS J. DOYLE, PAGES 74, 141, 172
ILLUSTRATIONS BY DAVE HELD PAGES 1, 35, 59, 185
PHOTOS COURTESY HISTORICAL SITES SOCIETY OF ARCATA
PAGES 166, 168, 169
PHOTOS BY KEVIN L. HOOVER, PAGES III, 26, 29, 43, 56, 58, 67 (R),
87, 94, 95, 97, 118, 148, 153
PHOTOS BY TERRENCE MCNALLY, PAGES 53, 55, 67 (L), 82, 171, 188
ILLUSTRATIONS BY LUSH NEWTON PAGES 98, 129, 191
ILLUSTRATIONS BY BOBBY WRIGHT PAGES 16, 157
COVER DESIGN AND ILLUSTRATIONS, BOOK DESIGN
BY PIXTON DUQUESNE
FLYING EYEBALLS COURTESY BRIAN SPROUL
BONGOS COURTESY WILDWOOD MUSIC
CREATED WITH APPLE MACINTOSH COMPUTERS

# FORBIDDEN FOREWORD

There are three wonderful things about the Police Log in the *Arcata Eye*, each more wonderful than the others. Allow me to mention four of them.

1. For the people who live outside the greater Arcata metro area, the Police Log provides an endlessly fascinating alternate universe, and a place with mysterious buildings – the Pink House – mysterious intersections – Ninth and H – and mysterious public amenities – Redwood Park. There is a glossary in the back of this book that provides actual definitions, but I like my fantasy Arcata better, a place where all the men are unsteady, all the women have issues and all the children know rather too much about organic produce.

Of course, that's not the complete picture of Arcata. The art form here is a police log, a standard feature in small town newspapers, so of necessity it represents the seamier side of life. There is an *Alice in Wonderland* kind of squalor, a Bukowski meets Thoreau sort of place, where old-fashioned hippie values encounter eternal human failings.

I suggest reading this book slowly, perhaps opening it at random. Perhaps you will enter the Plaza, a sort of 24-hour anti-AA meeting where people take turns standing up and saying, "Hi, my name's Pete, and I'm drunk," replacing "Pete" with their own names, usually. There is Samoa Boulevard, where there's often trouble a-brewin', and you might if you wish wonder why a wet and chilly California coastal town should name a street after a South Pacific island. Then there's the Intermodal Transient Facility, which, candidly, God only knows what *it* is.

And here's a tip for visitors to Arcata, straight from someone who's never been there: *Try to avoid the pizza parlor parking lot.*

2. The Police Log offers readers a unique opportunity to live the life of Kevin L. Hoover. Not Kevin L. Hoover, editor, reporter and family man, but "Kevin L. Hoover," the existential hero, the last moral man in a corrupt universe, walking the semi-mean streets of Arcata, observing without judging, except when he decides, the hell with it, I'm going to judge. The night falls like a quart of Jack Daniel's on a supermarket floor, the demons of the human heart prowl the streets like dogs prowling the streets. (Note to self: Better simile.)  Kevin L. Hoover sees it all. His eyes are as clear as the view from the vista point above the Sea of Tranquility, but his heart is as big as a graduation night hangover.

For instance, almost at random, this entry from the log:

• **Sunday, April 7 12:12 a.m.** He probably could have drawn an equally convincing ID with thrift shop Crayolas, and, probably, he should have.

Note the compassion. From just a little further down the page:

**4:25 p.m.**  A traveler positioned himself in front of an F Street pet shop and told passersby he was going to eat his dog.

Note the calm recitation of the surprising facts. And this, from a few pages further on:

• **Tuesday, April 16 2:01 p.m.** The cosmic statistical imperative dictates that there must be one lingering freak in every Arcata parking lot who just can't get it through his head that he isn't wanted there.

Note the philosophical approach. "More in sorrow than in

anger" – that's "Kevin L. Hoover" all over.

3. The Police Log contains some of the greatest prose this side of well, whoever you think writes good. A steady listing of petty crimes is a very limited form, almost like a haiku, but much can be made of it when it falls into the right hands. There are endless changes; there is mantric repetition. And, to spice up the individual items, there is sly wit and world-class phrase-making:

> • **Monday, December 17 8:12 a.m.** A guy in a white sweatshirt was reported outside the high school, directing students to where they could obtain that excellent fact-retention enabler, marijuana.

> • **New Year's Day 2002 11:25 a.m.** An underwear drawer may not offer the Fort Knox-like security one assumes, and certainly nothing approaching the sock drawer's vault-like impregnability. A Buttermilk Lane resident is out $300.

> **2:54 a.m.** Equipped with opposing thumb and forefinger, an ingrained hunter-gatherer species tradition and a crazy dream, a man entered a 24-hour supermarket and, say police, stuffed some animal parts under his jacket and fled the store. But he and his ill-gotten meat were quickly corralled in the 100 block of F Street, and he (the suspect) was arrested and jailed on a burglary charge and escorted to the Pink House. *Yo, what are you in for?* Boosted a car. *You?* Knocked over a gas station. *You?* Flank steak in my flannel.

One more gem. This is the kind of thing that a professional writer of periodical non-fiction writes and hardly thinks about, and then a day later thinks, "Damn, I was channeling greatness, and I didn't even know it." Then he gets up and kicks the wall joyfully. Then, since no one has noticed, he sits down, knowing the Pulitzer committee will never pay attention, even though they should:

> **2:55 p.m.** Hell, we all did stupid stuff when we were young.
>
> **3:30 p.m.** Oh, like *you're* perfect.
>
> **4:02 p.m.** Remember that time you got caught?
>
> **6:28 p.m.** Well *OK,* then.

4. Then there are the narratives themselves, the unexpected always cheek by jowl with the over-familiar. It's Peyton Place meets Samuel Beckett. Are all our lives just a series of tedious and repetitive thrusts into the ineffable terror of existence? Or do we just like to get loaded and partnered up, as did our ape forebears? These are questions that have puzzled the greatest philosophers. I've worried about them too.

There is an undercurrent of sadness in all this. Kevin L. Hoover has worked in Arcata (right near the Plaza, actually) for a number of years, and he has seen its calm and beauty distorted by human stupidity and cruelty. There are only so many "view with alarm" things a journalist can write about before its unchanging banality becomes unbearable.

Maybe one way to communicate that outrage is to ride on top of the waves, noting and commenting and holding up to ridicule. It demonstrates both compassion and contempt; it gives citizens a way to deal with the bad old world.

Perhaps there is no grace to be found here, but that doesn't mean we should stop looking. Follow along with Kevin L. Hoover, who cares enough to write it all down.

Jon Carroll
*October, 2004*

# SHOCKING
# AUTHOR'S NOTE

The sometimes surreal reality show that is Arcata, California regularly draws national, even global attention. Our little college town amid the redwood trees continues to foment fascination for its bleeding-edge politics, eco-grooviliciousness and the surreal reality show always in progress on its streets. Yes, this stuff really happened.

When you or I steal someone's blood pressure medicine, pee on shopping carts or have a yelling match at the car wash, we do so with a certain decorum which includes trying not to attract attention. But when others aren't so circumspect, their momentary lust for near-term gratification becomes government business and, subsequently, grist for the coplog. Then we can indulge our guilty pleasure, that piquant mix of voyeurism and *schadenfreude*, in reading about a moment of sneakiness made immortal.

It's not all fun and games for the cops, who have to deal with the serious crime that doesn't make it into these funny pages – violence in its many forms, children in jeopardy and people trapped by circumstance in unhappy life situations, to name a few. But the banality of evil is just as ably illustrated by a criminal mastermind leaning into a car's steering wheel and honking the horn while he struggles to pry the stereo loose from the dashboard.

Keep in mind too that most of the perps here aren't really bad people. Given that they've chosen to direct their might and main to the pursuit of, say, a frosty forty from a mini-mart, true evil is probably a bit beyond their budget.

Apparently people are going to just keep running down the street with tip jars, sleeping off another *bon vivant* evening under someone's porch and, in Arcata, pounding those unconscionable bongos. And we who've so far eluded capture will continue to muse about they who weren't so lucky.

Kevin L. Hoover
*November, 2004*

• **New Year's Day, 2001 12:27 – 4:22 a.m.** Several citizens were arrested and plopped in the Pink House on suspicion of miscellaneous threats to sobriety.

• **Saturday, January 6 4:43 p.m.** Today's astute stoner shouldn't chug the herb in the alley behind Tavern Row unless he has a fondness for government paperwork.

• **Tuesday, January 9 4:02 p.m.** His biological mother wishes for contact, and he doesn't.

**8:16 p.m.** Bio-mom was parked outside his house. An officer helped sever the emotional umbilicus.

• **Wednesday, January 10 1:27 p.m.** To a non-Arcatan, a shambling, giggling pile of blankets capped by a pertly arrayed headdress of clothing scraps both jaunty and grimy in equal measure compels police attention. John the policeman greeted Pete the Ragman in the 1400 block of H Street, and all was well.

**2:14 p.m.** An I Street business reverse-enjoyed a screwball visitation.

• **Thursday, January 11 3:31 p.m.** A traveler's route through earthly existence involved a little stroll in traffic at 11th near Union Street. He lived.

• **Friday, January 12 9:49 a.m.** There's no excuse for acting like that in a hospital cafeteria.

**10:43 a.m.** If you see any road signs in your kid's bedroom, you might inquire as to whether they came from Alliance Road and Stromberg Avenue.

**4:07 p.m.** A certain downtown corner lived up to its legend. Saggily clad hangabouts and their stringed companion animals moved along.

• **Saturday, January 13 12:38 a.m.** DUI, jailed.

**1:08 a.m.** DUI, jailed.

**2:34 a.m.** DUI, jailed.

**8:10 p.m.** DUI, jailed.

**9:20 p.m.** Just stay away from our San José-based investment consortium-owned shopping/profit center, OK?

**10:27 p.m.** Persons were observed kicking an undiscerned object at 10th and K streets. Police found naught but a thoroughly thrashed, handily humiliated and ignominiously abandoned water heater.

**10:52 p.m.** A young traveler at Ninth and H was de-cannabinized.

**11:02 p.m.** A Ninth and H sidewalk socialite was drunk tanked.

**• Monday, January 15 7:14 p.m.** An Olympia Streeter fully charged with life's exuberance, at a minimum, was reported cursing, banging and playing loud, loud music. He agreed to attempt subtlety.

**7:57 p.m.** Roommate life certainly has its ups and downs. The real downs tend to involve conversations with uniformed personnel.

**8:40 p.m.** Men were reportedly brawling in a Valley West motel's parking lot. Actually, it was an ugly exercise in good citizenship – a bunch of fellas were trying to remove a wiped-out pal from a bar and take him home with all organs and appendages still connected and throbbing.

**10:42 p.m.** A too-young Eurekan was arrested at an adult social estab on charges of being a minor on the premises, probation violation, public drunkenness and fussing during the arrest procedure. A pink fortress in his home town contained that bad boy.

**• Tuesday, January 16 3:38 p.m.** While being either brown or a Dodge would instantly trigger suspicion of any van that was possibly selling controlled substances in the parking lot of a cooperative supermarket on the 800 block of I Street, this vehicle was both. When police arrived, it was uninhabited.

**• Wednesday, January 17 1:12 p.m.** Pete and a manifestly mislabeled fellow name of Lucky were cited and released on a chump charge of camping at the Veteran's Hall.

**• Thursday, January 18 5:07 a.m.** As chaos reigned in

PG&E's boardroom, its shock troops went about maintaining the infrastructure even if there was no juice to pump through it, mending a downed line at 12th and O streets.

**11:10 a.m.** Phone calls yielded no result, and the letters didn't help either. Finally, police were called in by a Valley West full-service supermarket in a last-ditch effort to jiggle loose two rented videos from a Grotzman Road resident. Officers delivered the complaint.

**2:09 p.m.** Pedestrians-be-damned oblivioids skateboarded at Ninth and H streets.

**5:20 p.m.** An astute observer noted that stop signs, including the one at California Avenue and Evergreen Lane, function somewhat less than optimally when horizontal.

• **Saturday, January 20 9:43 p.m.** Janes Road is actually *not* a motorcycle drag strip – news to this one guy, who garaged his wheels at the revelation.

• **Sunday, January 21 12:48 – 12:53 a.m.** Suspected drunk drivers arrested on Alliance Road and in Stewart Court next had the opportunity to pilot the indestructible stainless steel integrated toilet/sink combo appliance in the Pink House drunk tank cell.

**11:20 a.m.** A woman made a nuisance of herself at a downtown coffee temple, and was go-awayed.

**2:51 p.m.** The she-nuisance was deemed unsuitable for a Plaza liquor store.

**3:04 p.m.** Another naif learned the folly of leaving a purse in an unlocked car, yes, even in friendly Sunny Brae.

**3:16 p.m.** A woman was detained for psych eval along Tavern

Row, then taken to the bin for storage.

**5:16 p.m.** Couple indestructibility with a thirst for fun and the only logical thing to do is hang over the side of the Samoa Boulevard/U.S. Highway 101 overpass. Two youths were admonished.

**10:24 p.m.** An Alliance Road resident reported cows mooing and a popping sound like a BB gun, and the imagination reels with possibilities. But an officer found no cows and no odd sounds.

• **Monday, January 22 11:38 a.m.** The Old Arcata Road owner of a large, aggressive dog read a note left by an APD officer when he returned home later this day.

• **Friday, January 26 12:52 p.m.** Ryan the traveler set up his tent in Shay Park's micro-wilderness, but had to take it down and leave sooner than he'd anticipated.

**4:48 p.m.** A traveler entered a Plaza office building demanding to use the bathroom, and wouldn't take no for an answer. When he voiced rather piquant character insights regarding the building's employees, police were called and relocated him to the Pink House on a public intox charge.

**6:51 p.m.** A downtown professional enjoyed one of the perks of an Arcata worklife – being able to walk from home to office, meeting and greeting friends and familiar sights along the way. But as he neared the core of downtown, his fortunes turned as the already-narrow walkway turned into an obstacle course in front of an H Street restaurant. There, he said, two percussionists performed a drum duet, facing each other across the narrow sidewalk. As the pedestrian wended his way carefully between the bongoists, he grazed – at most, nudged – one of the musicians' hand drums. At that, the drummer became dramatist, mortally stricken that anyone would invade his space so brazenly, and rose to his feet as if to mount a physical challenge to the innocent passerby. "You mean you want to *fight* me over this?" asked the bongo nudger, who just walked on. Down the way, he was briefly blocked again by a bicyclist who rolled up, stopped in his path and said "That was my friend!" Again the challenge was sidestepped, and the fellow somehow made his way to work without further incident.

**7:29 p.m.** Noisoids outside a Plaza bar agreed to quiet down.

**• Saturday, January 27 12:35 a.m.** A pro-Democracy rally held on the Plaza included speakers unintentionally replicating the posture of reviled dead white male Mr. Wm. McKinley. Also interesting were the plum tree branches which had been ripped from seven of the trees surrounding the Plaza's inner circle and artfully arranged at Big Bill's base. Protesters vigorously denied any connection with the display, which seemed to carry an implicit warning that new restrictions of downtown behavior would not be imposed without retaliation. But as it turned out, the amputated limbs were the alleged handiwork of a Florida man who had suffered a reversal of fortune in a billiards game at a nearby social estab early the previous Saturday morning and took it out on the trees. The pruner without portfolio was plucked from the Plaza and promptly Pink-plopped.

**1:19 a.m.** Direct Action – the humiliation of a Giuntoli Lane beverage vending machine – brought corporate America to its knees.

**3:15 a.m.** Another beverage machine was humiliated in the 2200 block of Alliance Road, apparently in the service of one person's interlocking obsessive-compulsive disorder and sublimated rage condition.

**3:38 a.m.** A locking gas cap would have assured a Valley West woman better mileage, as her tank was drained by petrol pirates.

• **Tuesday, January 30 1:56 a.m.** Sidewalk slouchers reportedly blocked the sidewalk at Ninth and H streets. Police herded the millabouts out of the way.

• **Wednesday, January 31 4 a.m.** A religious worship facility on 11th Street provided neither spiritual succor nor shelter for two campers, who were warned about camping and trespass regs and sent on their way.

**7:28 p.m.** A mental meltdown victim was transferred from a Plaza liquor store to the bin.

• **Wednesday, February 7 12:09 p.m.** A Granite Avenue resident left his car unlocked, and now drives in silence.

**1:49 p.m.** A guy who has adopted nibbling at the fringes of a downtown office building as a way of life panhandled people using the ATM, then slumped away.

**5 p.m.** Jason the traveler (they're all named Jason, mostly) was arrested on a public drunkenness charge (they're not all drunk, mostly) at Ninth and H streets.

• **Friday, February 9 5:51 a.m.** A liquor-pickled soul parked in a pickup truck in a downtown lot was arrested and drunk tanked.

• **Saturday, February 10 6:19 a.m.** There's always something to argue about – even if it's nothing – on South G Street, at virtually any hour.

**4:05 p.m.** Ninth and H'ers shared stinkarette smoke with passersby.

• **Monday, February 12 3:15 p.m.** Possessions such as cell phones which enter locker rooms with one person sometimes leave with another.

• **Thursday, February 15 5:27 p.m.** His gaze probably locked on the green light at Samoa Boulevard and H streets, a tow truck driver with a gold or brown car on the back zoomed through the stop-signed intersection of Seventh and H streets at, oh, 25 to 30 miles per hour. You aren't supposed to do that. Caltrans is re-doing the Samoa and H juncture – maybe they'll install signals that don't beckon southbound drivers to floor it from the Plaza. *[Late update – they didn't, and they still do – Ed.]*

**10:46 p.m.** A man stood in the intersection of Hilfiker Drive and Baldwin Street and yelled "murder!" This aroused suspicion for some reason, but the guy was gone on police arrival.

**10:47 p.m.** Someone bounced, bounced, bounced, bounced a basketball continuously on Chester Avenue long enough to wake up neighbors, then left.

• **Friday, February 16 1:43 a.m.**
A driver found cocktail savaged
With motoring skills of a cabbage
Was moved from the wheel
To behind bars of steel
Where his kidneys could work to advantage.

**4:14 p.m.** The term "defrauding an innkeeper" may evoke enchanting images of adventure and romance in medieval times – mammoth mutton legs washed down with pungent grog from a pewter chalice; furtive rolls in the hay with a country maiden; swashbuckling escapes on a hastily conscripted steed... but in this case, a Rio Deller allegedly scarfed down some deli fare and boogied from a 13th Street marketplace. She was cited, booked and released.

**8:03 p.m.** Eric next surfaced in regard to a little shoplifting mix-up at an I Street cooperative supermarket. Jail – a place where one may linger with impunity.

• **Sunday, February 18 2:03 a.m.** An alley gladiator was Pink Housed.

**7:45 p.m.** "Could ya kick down a couple of coins and help us out, *myaaan*?" beseeched the feeb at the ATM in a full-blown marijuana accent. The cannabinoid cadger had shuffled randomly off in a macro-scale demonstration of Brownian Motion when police arrived.

**10:44 p.m.** Someone stole the Ninth and H sign.

• **Tuesday, February 20 1:58 a.m.** Three guys did a scarf 'n' scram at a Janes Road 24-hour corporate greasery.

**1:04 p.m.** Ninth and H sidewalk sitters had become vertical when the forces of oppression arrived.

• **Wednesday, February 21 1:25 a.m.**
A traveler who sells pipes of glass
To those on the Plaza who pass
Had merchandise ripped
By one alleged dip
Cops tracked down and busted his ass.

**12:05 p.m.** Two travelers tried to shout their way to a better world at the Intermodal Transient Facility. It didn't work.

**2:58 p.m.** Weirdo alert at a downtown office building.

**4:24 p.m.** Sitabouts badgered customers in front of a bar near the Ninth and H youth activity center, then bailed.

**6:53 p.m.** Hoping to streamline the journey of cash from the bank accounts of passersby into their pockets, two travelers set up a panhandling station at a Plaza ATM. An officer discouraged the enterprise.

• **Saturday, February 24 8:46 a.m.** How much did she really *want* her purse, if she left it in an unlocked car at 11th and A streets?

• **Wednesday, February 28 9:48 a.m.** Petrol pirates drained a tank in the 500 block of J Street.

**9:28 p.m.** The aural equivalent of water torture – a bouncing basketball – bestirred a call to police from the 1500 block of Chester Avenue.

**9:40 p.m.** Incorrigible snoozer Pete took another nap alongside a restaurant in the 300 block of G Street.

• **Friday, March 2 2:10 a.m.** Thank you, Officer Stonebarger, for removing this unsteady individual from behind the wheel and repositioning him behind bars.

**4:20 a.m.** Thank you, Officer Gatty, for removing this unlicensed, uninsured, unregistered, fake-ID'd individual from behind the wheel and repositioning him behind bars.

**9:43 p.m.** I'll be waiting for you outside when you get off work, promised a surly countenance. The employee got a police escort outta there.

**9:57 p.m.** A traveler was arrested along Tavern Row for alleged cocktail jubilation.

**10:26 p.m.** Unforgivable inroads on personal liberty were inflicted on a traveler who was cited for drinking and dogging downtown.

• **Wednesday, March 7 11:35 p.m.** Another ordinance

ignorer was warned for doin' the dog along Tavern Row.

• **Thursday, March 8 12:39 a.m.** A groundscore consisting of a bag full of marijuana plants just lying there on the St. Louis Road overpass fell into unappreciative hands – those of the police.

**10:20 p.m.** Fists exchanged views in front of a Northtown coffee house. One combatant scampered over the ped walkway. Another lingered and failed the fingertip-to-nose challenge. Pinked.

• **Friday, March 9 3:10 p.m.** A youth's alleged quest to rip off hooch from an F Street variety store took a detour through Juvenile Hall.

• **Monday, March 12 10:40 a.m.** The mayor of a small coastal college town reported a dog running loose on the town square, where children play and people eat, or would like to. An Animal Control officer warned the owner.

**7:43 p.m.** A skater was warned about appropriating the flower beds at the corner of Ninth and G streets for his personal show-off quest, which effectively excluded use and enjoyment of the public facility by all others other than those who are impressed by the display of falling-down derring-do. An officer what's-upped the kid and access was restored.

**11:08 p.m.** Florida guy and Texas gal argued over whatever. She was arrested on charges of drunk driving and child endangerment, and jailed.

• **Wednesday, March 14 6:52 p.m.** Chet the traveler was deemed just the sort of drunk guy the Pink House was made for.

• **Friday, March 16 10:41 a.m.** Someone stole a pane of glass from a home in the 100 block of G Street.

**3:02 p.m.** A Plaza employee reported someone throwing clothing on his car.

**3:19 p.m.** A nug vendor at Eighth and H streets needs better demographic research.

• **Tuesday, March 20 1:04 – 2:20 a.m.** You can't get a decent night's car sleep in this town, from Valley West Boulevard to South G Street to 11th Street and the freeway.

**3:59 p.m.** An arrogant television network helicopter buzzed Fifth and J streets, collecting footage of Arcataland for a TV show.

• **Wednesday, March 21 4:07 p.m.** A runaway young person located at the Intermodal Transit Facility was turned over to youth authorities to be returned from the Fabled Land of Humboldt to Milpitas.

• **Thursday, March 22 12:17 a.m.** A dream roommate was reported having stolen a cohabitant's cash and "tainted" his food in some manner better left undescribed.

**9:38 a.m.** Fecal coliform donors discovered behind the Redwood Lodge were rustled on outta there.

**12:43 p.m.** Ponder, if you will, the utter banality of a restraining order.

**6:25 p.m.** Another entrepreneur's business plan involved going door to door offering firewood for sale, then getting all pissy when people declined to purchase his woody wares.

• **Friday, March 23 11:35 a.m.** Flower planters are for skateboarding, you fascist.

**11:34 p.m.** A Foster Avenue resident reported youths picking up rocks from Shay Park and announcing their intention to smash windshields with them, but the braggadocio proved vacuous.

• **Saturday, March 24 4:12 a.m.** Police concluded that there was no legit reason for a local man to be carrying burglary tools in the 200 block of 12th Street, so they took them away from him and put him in jail.

**9:31 p.m.** Alleged possession of marijuana and a controlled substance did not, in an officer's view, compensate for having a suspended license. A driver was transplanted from the 1600 block of I Street to Big Pink.

• **Sunday, March 25 2:03 a.m.** A cocktail-dizzied charmer with outstanding warrants both moistened and fertilized the 700 block of Eighth Street. Off to the Pink House.

**8:37 p.m.** A guest to our town, suffused with the excitement of Arcata's vibrant downtown nightlife, and booze, was moved from Ninth and H streets to the Pink House.

• **Wednesday, March 28 2:10 p.m.** Sidewalk wallowers impeded someone's lifestyle from proceeding undetoured at Ninth and H. Two sitabouts briefly approached linear thought patterns during an interlude with an officer.

**3:12 p.m.** The dumpster at an H Street cannabis center holds unusual appeal for some. What, like they just toss out dank buds? A traveler found on an ill-fated dumpster spelunking expedition denied all, but was advised and warned.

**3:12 p.m.** Low frequencies conduct especially well through structure, so one man's righteous bass line became a neighboring woman's rumbling nightmare. Somewhere, a volume knob twirled counter-clockwise.

• **Thursday, March 29 2:16 a.m.** Had they not been lodged

in separate, gender-specific quarters at the Pink House, Party Beast might have gotten on well with a woman arrested on a drunk driving charge in the 1200 block of G Street.

**3:11 p.m.** Two males were reported making a stump out of a tree at the intersection of Trails 1 and 2.

• **Friday, March 30 12:57 p.m.** Five lingerators at Ninth and H were motivated.

**6:26 p.m.** A woman reported three boys throwing an orange and profanity at her at 11th and H streets.

**7:59 p.m.** A traveler was cited for having a dog that didn't seem to be going anywhere downtown.

• **Sunday, April 1 6:16 p.m.** Consistent with the new vogue in driving, a motorist blew the stop sign at 10th and H streets.

• **Monday, April 2 5:24 p.m.** Dingbats quibbled at high volume in a downtown parking lot.

**7:45 p.m.** Hey, hang on to my guitar for me till I get out, OK?

**9:55 p.m.** A Plaza barkeep complained of sidewalk sluggards, who overcame cannabinoid paralysis and reluctantly motated except for one dude, a traveler, scooped up and Pinked on warrants.

• **Tuesday, April 3 1:11 p.m.** Had the alleged doper at the Ball Park been as smart as them dogs, he too might have eluded a citation.

**4:44 p.m.** They shouldn't make new buildings at Seventh and F with so-sweet skating surfaces if they don't want wheeled young men to utilize same.

• **Wednesday, April 4 12:21 a.m.** Another alcohol-flavored chap outside a downtown bar was cop-scooped and Pink-plopped.

**3:28 a.m.** The generic, anywhere-in-America architecture of a Plaza bank was not particularly improved by graffiti scrawlings.

**11:58 a.m.** No driver's license, no insurance, no seat belts.

**12:35 p.m.** Two dope-dizzied travelers were separated from their prized herb stash at 13th and F streets.

**3:14 p.m.** A traveler previously cited for smoking on the corner of Ninth and H streets had denied being a tobacco aficionado, but there he was smoking again. Where is truth?

**3:24 p.m.** A frequent flyer again went south, in more ways than one, courtesy Pink House Jailways.

**4:20 p.m.** Three coin-begging sitabouts at Ninth and G were blued.

**• Thursday, April 5 1:21 a.m.** The fire suppression valve and lock boxes at a Northtown medical clinic were damaged by someone who needs a hobby, or a different hobby.

**8:13 a.m.** The story of humanity was little augmented by the dust-up between a he and she at the Intermodal Transient Facility. Inexplicably embargoing vital factoids which we might use to judge them, Danny the traveler couldn't remember what the argument was about, and the lady of the manor wouldn't say her name or give any other info.

**4:14 p.m.** When construction finally begins at Ninth and H, jackhammer music will effectively prevent this sort of thing.

**6:45 p.m.** Contrition and reparations followed a scarf 'n' scram at a downtown cornucopia of delights and arterial plaque buildup for young and old.

**11:36 p.m.** Would that we could all know the Steinbeckian tales of road life undoubtedly stored in the memory banks of Jed, Jason and Michael, travelers all.

• **Saturday, April 7 12:27 a.m.** Sitting in his van on the Plaza, someone placed a marijuana pipe in a guy's hand, said the innocent THC victim, and he turned his head to see a policeman greeting him through the window. A citation followed.

**2:59 p.m.** Reports flooded in of numerous loose cows on South F Street. They amiably hoofed it back to their pasture to be fattened up for eventual execution and dismemberment.

**5:39 p.m.** A heretic was excommunicated from a downtown coffee temple.

• **Monday, April 9 11:03 a.m.** Another heathen cast out of a downtown coffee temple.

**5:02 p.m.** More hippie clottage at Ninth and H.

• **Tuesday, April 10 9:35 a.m.** Pete took a dump in someone's yard and was citizen arrested, then cited.

**2:47 p.m.** Three unsecured dogs in the back of a pickup truck bark-startled walkers-by, earning their owner a little briefing on City dog ordinances.

• **Wednesday, April 11 3:26 p.m.** Yelling like that in the 600 block of F Street gets people out of a shopping mood real quick, and this will not be tolerated.

**5:49 p.m.** A traveler was arrested at Ninth and H on on charges of excessive bloodstream liquor buildup and resisting arrest, and sent Pinkward.

• **Saturday, April 14 8:50 a.m.** Pete and his latest drinking buddy perched on someone's back porch in the 1300 block of H Street and took to guzzling. An officer counseled motation. Pete shambled, but that was good enough.

**10:21 a.m.** A mouth-breather at the controls of a paintball gun had the inspiration to take a potshot at a home near Redwood Park after expending the bulk of his ammo in the natural splendor of Arcata's redwood cathedral.

**3:30 p.m.** There's many a dip who puts bottle to lip in an otherwise wholesome downtown parking lot.

**7:12 p.m.** Smokin' and drinkin' at Ninth and H.

**8:38 p.m.** There's a lot to bark at on Golf Course Road.

**10:22 p.m.** A raccoon did a pretty good burglar imitation on California Avenue, rattling around in a garage.

• **Sunday, April 15 12:49 p.m.** A car theft was reported at Westwood Center.

**5:28 p.m.** Guys being guys on a late Sunday afternoon on the roof of a Charles Avenue home were asked to quieten down.

• **Monday, April 16 4:56 a.m.** Three travelers were contacted in their groovy nomadic vehicle on Alliance Road, and were briefed on portions of the Arcata Municipal Code regulating urban camping.

**3:25 p.m.** Cars doinked at Ninth and F streets, and their pilots bickered in the street. No transcript is available.

• **Tuesday, April 17 9:05 a.m.** In only five minutes, conditions at City Hall had set one guy to yellin'. He scampered.

**6:42 p.m.** Isn't it great to live in a place where loose cows in the roadway are still a problem?

**11:05 p.m.** Maybe in West Covina they park in red fire zones, but not on Crescent Way in Sunny Brae, *uh-uh.*

• **Wednesday, April 18 12:18 a.m.** On the scale of wilderness camping experiences, the back lot of a corporate supermarket butted up against the freeway is challenged in glamour only by the shelter offered by the underpass abutment just over the fence. Two discerning travelers moved along to more elegant quarters, which would be almost anywhere.

**6:46 a.m.** Pete got in some kinda trouble of the alcoholic kind at a minor movie theater on H Street. He went to a place where they know him well.

**8:43 p.m.** A Hawaiian got arrested for obstruction and false information – sterile terms no doubt masking a far richer experience – on the Plaza. He went to jail in a cloudy place.

• **Thursday, April 19 12:24 a.m.** A report of a man mumbling in the 100 block of H Street drew police interest. A traveler summoned up what articulation he could, augmented by emphatic hand motions, to decline assistance.

**2:10 a.m.** A treacherous cretin humiliated a car antenna at an Alliance Road stop 'n' rob.

**2:27 a.m.** Representatives of an advanced race of alcohol-consuming creatures were next arrested in the alley of adventure, shackled and impounded in an earthling incarceration facility.

**10:28 a.m.** Out, out, damn Spot, an illegally stationary dog in the downtown area. A traveler was cited and released.

**10:38 a.m.** A loved one had passed on, and there, at Ninth and H streets, a man broke down and wept.

**10:46 a.m.** Engorged with adult beverages, say police, a traveler was arrested in City Hall and jailed.

**1:10 p.m.** Three travelers were warned about doing illegal things with their bongos on the Plaza. Like playing them.

**3:13 p.m.** A mayor reported nug merchants plying their, like, craft on the Plaza. They scuttled like roaches.

**3:41 p.m.** A traveler at 12th and M streets learned more than he ever wanted to know about Arcata's camping laws, then forgot it.

**5:03 p.m.** Two travelers were arrested on theft charges at an I Street cooperative supermarket, one for allegedly lying to the cops. They soon kept company with drunks in an echoey government building. The warrant check turned up a surprise, and then there was the pot.

• **Saturday, April 21 6:14 a.m.** Travelers Melissa, Joseph,

David, Trina, Sebastian, George, Wade, Brian, Mabel and Travis were cited for camping in the Redwood Park fecal coliform incubator.

**4:41 p.m.** A person was reported "with a dog smoking" on the Plaza, but both master and his nicotine-dependent pooch were gone on police arrival.

**8:35 p.m.** Someone stole the mayor's purse from the Community Center.

• **Sunday, April 22 4:56 a.m.** A hitchhiker was found yelling and screaming obscenities on the southbound onramp at U.S. Highway 101 at Sunset Avenue, maybe just to keep warm.

**6:25 p.m.** A puny sinkhole reverse-erupted in the 1000 block of C Street. It was coned and Public Works contacted.

• **Tuesday, April 24 10:25 a.m.** Ninth and H'ers went on a tear, first trying to knock down the street sign, then peeing on a wall and finally utilizing a nearby carport utility room for recreational activities.

**4:33 a.m.** A locked-out resident's beseechments to an unresponsive roommate penetrated the lodgings of adjacent tenants at an Alliance Road apartment complex. A woman agreed to quieten down and try again later.

**3 p.m.** If you were a loose dog in a world of asphalt and right angles, you'd hang out at the fragrant bagel shop too.

• **Thursday, May 24 1:54 a.m.** Another soul somehow became locked inside a downtown storehouse after closing time, and was released.

**3:59 a.m.** Another yap-happy pooch on West End Road.

**6:31 p.m.** An alleged shoplifter was arrested at an I Street cooperative supermarket carrying a switchblade knife, an armament all out of proportion to that needed to secure tofu.

• **Friday, May 25 1:48 a.m.** A Trinidude was arrested on a charge of transferring excessive amounts of adult beverage from bottle to gullet and resisting arrest, then Pink Housed.

**12:02 p.m.** Another soul sundered by demon weed at the Intermodal Transient Facility. He got a ticket.

• **Saturday, May 26 12:43 p.m.** Why would anyone refuse to leave a 13th Street marketplace when he was so plainly not wanted there? *Why?*

• **Sunday, May 27 12:27 a.m.** Someone stole some of the merchandise left out front of an F Street variety store, then ran away knowing that what he had done was so very wrong.

• **Monday, May 28 3:08 a.m.** What Haig Patigian and George Zehndner wrought, a mere vandal managed to sully. But McKinley's bronze effigy survives, resolute and unbesmirched, standing watch over the bustle and haste.

**5:23 p.m.** Participants in a food fight at Ninth and H streets agreed to clean up the mess. At least the food didn't go to waste.

• **Thursday, May 31 12:30 a.m.** Tears followed an argument.

**3:30 a.m.** Distraught over the death of her man, a woman wept.

**11:46 a.m.** Marijuana was removed from a traveler's possession, quite possibly saving him from a life of despair.

**1:26 p.m.** A woman was arrested on a charge of cocktailification in the 1600 block of Old Arcata Road, and delivered to the Pink Palace.

**2:51 p.m.** Three travs were arrested in Redwood Park on charges of possessing mindbending subs, and jailed.

**3:55 p.m.** A fellow who was altogether too insistent that small metallic discs in others' pockets be transferred to his at Samoa Boulevard and G Street was motivated to move along, move along.

• **Sunday, June 3 10:08 p.m.** A traveler at an F Street supermarket was arrested, booked and lodged in the always-accommodating Pink House on a public drunkitude charge. On searching him, they found that other stuff.

• **Monday, June 4 11:55 a.m.** Two travelers were cited and released for possession of a drug so wonderful, it offers not just squinty eyes, insatiable munchies, its own fashions, hairstyle, accent, philosophy and folklore, but unwanted government attention, too, at the Intermodal Transient Facility.

**12:33 a.m.** A traveler was arrested on charges of having concentrated cannabis (hash) and some pot for sale. Pinked on charges of Wonderment possession.

**8 a.m.** Possible Wonder Drug activity was reported at Ninth and H, but none was observed. What, like they'd still be nug-slinging when the cruiser rolled up?

**12:30 p.m.** Still another trav busted for alleged wonderment and Pinked at the ITF.

**1:08 p.m.** A local yokel was arrested on outstanding misdemeanor and infraction warrants in Valley West. And the commodious/odious Pink House absorbed another soul.

**1:08 p.m.** Police didn't believe this local woman really needed that controlled substance and a syringe. So much so that they stashed her in the Pink House.

**1:31 p.m.** Big Pink's burgeoning ranks further swelled with the addition of a local chap arrested on a charge of disobeying a court order.

**1:41 p.m.** A trav at Ninth and H was Pinked on a charge of disobeying a court order. Then they found his stash.

**2:47 p.m.** It's legal to smoke corporate-rolled cancer-causers, but not on the Plaza. A traveler got a ticket.

• **Wednesday, June 6 12:35 p.m.** A young woman of unknown address was cited for possession of the wonder drug.

**3:08 p.m.** A local man was cited for putting things in his pocket and leaving an I Street cooperative supermarket without giving the workers there money.

**3:43 p.m.** A he and she came to blows – the fighty kind – outside a Plaza tavern.

**4:15 p.m.** A person came to blows – the cigarette kind – on the Plaza, and was warned.

• **Friday, June 8 6:12 a.m.** A San Franciscan greeted the morning face down on the pavement in front of an I Street cooperative supermarket. Asked to move along, he did.

• **Sunday, June 10 12:03 a.m.** If your children were hanging around in the Tavern Row alley, you'd probably be pretty happy that the cops found them.

**12:55 a.m.** A local guy personally moistened that selfsame alley.

**1:14 a.m.** Oh, demon alcohol.

**2:15 a.m.** Sad memories I can't recall.

**2:21 a.m.** Who thought that I would fall?

**2:41 a.m.** Driven to demon alcohol!

**2:41 a.m.** Others prefer smokable brain teasers.

**12:40 a.m.** A guy in a blue van, the like of which has been heard to blurt *Uncle Meat* at odd hours, weirded someone out at the Marsh. An officer made his acquaintance.

**4:21 p.m.** She keeps hassling me, went one guy's version.

**6:10 p.m.** Three travelers convened at the Marsh where G and H street meet, and well, things got a little loud.

• **Monday, June 11 4:08 p.m.** A passerby reported someone lying on the sidewalk at Ninth and H. A traveler was sent on his way, on the assumption he has one of those.

• **Tuesday, June 12 4:40 a.m.** In the 500 block of G Street, layabout leisurites lounged loudly on a loading dock, perhaps trying to say that three times fast. An outdoorsman was warned regarding unlawful lodging.

• **Wednesday, June 13 3:30 p.m.** A skateboarder has had his way with the Plaza planters, then rolled away, fell, rolled, fell, etc. noisily.

• **Thursday, June 14 1:07 p.m.** It wasn't much of a contest, that skirmish between a large delivery van and the bicycle chained to a lightpost at 11th and H streets. An officer left a note on the bike's contorted remains.

**3:15 p.m.** A man reported his vehicle missing from 10th and G streets, but then this light bulb came on over his head and he made an embarrassed exit to where he had actually parked the car.

**4:03 p.m.** A traveling woman took a stealthy squat in Tavern Row, but was caught and ticketed by he known as Robocop.

• **Friday, June 15 1:35 a.m.** A canine choir on Baldwin Street was removed from the aria.

**1:49 a.m.**
A traveler at Ninth and I
Was schnockered, said the *polizei*
They probed his pockets, checked his pouch
And found, they said, his reefer – *ouch!*

**6:15 a.m.** A trusting soul left his car unlocked at the foot of California Street, and the rest, like his property, is history.

**8:56 a.m.** Campers Greg and Doreen roosted at a Samoa Boulevard barbecue restaurant. It was made clear that they were unwanted there, especially when self-marinating their brains with booze, and they wobbled away.

**3:32 p.m.** A traveler serenaded McKinley with consonant-rich discourse following a spat with this other dude.

**7:35 p.m.** I'm so mad at my mother.

**11:58 p.m.**
Two trav'lers were easily collared
At the bus station where they had hollered
Offending the ear
Of a resident near
Perhaps due to hooch that they'd swallered.

• **Sunday, June 17 8:46 – 10:45 – 11:11 a.m.** Feraliens

smoked their stink near public buildings, camped and used the place as a dog run. Exalt the noble savages for bringing down Babylon so effectively.

**7:35 p.m.** A grooving lifestyle more or less mandates ownership of one or more dogs, and if personal convenience requires that the pooches be confined to a car in the 1600 block of H Street all day, well, that's *their* problem.

**Pete liked his picture in the first Police Log book.**

• **Wednesday, June 20 11:19 a.m.** Pete and a pal *du jour* went to the Pink House on a probation violation charge.

**5:07 p.m.** A Kansas man reported something weird at Redwood Park. What do we have that *wouldn't* be weird to someone from Totoland?

**6 p.m.** The District Attorney is reviewing a case of offensive words deployed against a woman on Hallen Drive.

• **Thursday, June 21 2:09 a.m.** An all-nite party in the 500 block of G Street was enjoyed by all, except for uninvited neighbors who had jobs to go to the next day.

**7:40 a.m.** A concerned citizen reported the bat having flown around Council Chambers the previous night, but it had winged well away by then.

**4:48 p.m.** HSU police reported children possibly throwing things into freeway traffic from the 17th Street pedestrian overhead. An Arcata officer watched the kids motioning at cars below to honk. He hailed the honk harvesters.

**10:11 p.m.** *Bang!* Grotzman Road.

**11:37 p.m.** *Bang!* Cedar Drive.

• **Friday, June 22 2:18 a.m.** The party was just breaking up as police arrived. Coincidence? One wonders.

**4:05 a.m.** A narco-alky combo in the cheap apartments, said police.

**12:04 p.m.** Fancy that – pot at the transient facility.

**5:18 p.m.** Interpersonal drama flared – where else? – at the car wash, where bathos and auto-bathing flow like oily suds.

**7:10 p.m.** An apartment dweller at a Union Street residential inn reported someone smoking marijuana nearby. But the toker had a license to partake of the herb, was within legal limits, and that was that.

**9:23 p.m.** A traveler occupied the thin sidewalk outside a Northtown business for more than an hour. Apart from all the attendant civil liberties issues, the mystery remains – in a town with two dozen parks, why would anyone choose to wallow in spit and grime on a busy, narrow sidewalk?

• **Saturday, June 23 4:04 p.m.** Free-range solipsists appropriated the center of the Plaza for dubious hobbycraft, which centered around smoking and howling obscenities. A traveler was cited for prohibited puffing.

**9:45 p.m.** A burglar alarm sounded at a Giuntoli Lane animal clinic. Two loose dogs were found merrily padding about inside the business.

• **Tuesday, June 26 12:02 a.m.** A fire started in the fabled pile of oily rags in the 2500 block of Davis Way.

**12:11 a.m.** The Dollar Tree store reported a counterfeit bill, denomination undisclosed.

**3:10 p.m.** Three Aggro McSpangers were shooed away from an upscale H Street eatery/bar.

• **Wednesday, June 27 2:50 a.m.** A tree limb attacked a car at J and 15th streets, motive unknown.

**2:55 p.m.** Hell, we all did stupid stuff when we were young.

**3:30 p.m.** Oh, like *you're* perfect?

**4:02 p.m.** Remember that time you got caught?

**6:28 p.m.** Well *OK,* then.

• **Thursday, June 28 2:11 a.m.** Astaire and Rogers. Lennon and McCartney. Booze and pot.

**2:12 a.m.** Their love ended. She cried.

**8:10 a.m.** "Rethink patriotism," urged the graffiti on the fireworks stand at Eighth and H streets. The stand was later burglarized by those who may have done so and reached alternative conclusions.

**2:27 p.m.** The music-consuming public accepts and expects percussion, yet, anomalously, is keenly intolerant of those practicing to get good at it, this time on Ross Street.

**Alfred Edmunson**

• **Friday, June 29 10:16 a.m.** Alfred the signholder at 17th and G was reported yelling at passing traffic. But it was actually in the spirit of public service – he told an officer he was yelling at a driver who had failed to stop at a stop sign.

**3:12 p.m.** More court-bound spark at Ninth and H.

• **Saturday, June 30 1:35 a.m.** Needless to say, Mom and Dad weren't pleased at being called to the station at this hour.

**2:58 a.m.** A traveler cracked open a refreshing adult beverage at the Intermodal Transient Facility, and was all too soon signing official paperwork.

**5:34 p.m.** A traveler reportedly tried to make a hardscrabble home in Shay Park.

**9:44 p.m.** A traveler was cited and released for having an open container along Tavern Row, but mere moments later...

**10:06 p.m.** ...the same Captain Clueless, obviously in dire need of a cost/benefit analysis, was cited and released again for drinking at Ninth and H.

• **Sunday, July 1 12:07 a.m.** A too-fake I.D. ill-served an El

Centro man at a Plaza night spot.

**12:31 a.m.** A new kid in town was Pinked after a slappy spat in the piss-glistened alley behind Tavern Row.

**4:31 a.m.** No, we didn't build this nature interpretive center for you to sleep and poop upon.

**6:31 p.m.** A traveler reported his money stolen somewhere downtown. If you see it, call police.

**8:09 p.m.** I'll lean here if I want, reported the sullen, shiftless figure in front of a Plaza business. But a mere phone call effected his evacuation.

**9:10 p.m.** Ripoff reptiles slithered through a car parked at 10th and H streets.

**• Monday, July 2 9:35 p.m.** If your friend tied you to a tree in the G Street alley behind the Plaza, would their leaving you a bowl of water make it OK? A dog's unconditional love was undimmed by the incident.

**• Tuesday, July 3 5:16 a.m.** Stores have little choice but to leave their garden wares outside overnight, gambling that, simply put, *what kind of chump would mess with vegetable starts?* Chumps do.

**3:11 p.m.** Another best friend imprisoned with a bowl of water in a parked vehicle – this one at the Intermodal Transient Facility – as the owner gallivanted insouciantly about town.

**4:34 p.m.** When it's over, it's over. One half of the relationship was slow to embrace this concept.

**• Fourth of July 3:18 – 3:21 a.m.** Various stupidity-based exploits helped swell the Pink House's population, to the probable detriment of its average I.Q.

**7:37 a.m.** When these particular people decide to get along, police logs will require a lot less paper.

**11:48 a.m.** Pot, hash and jail.

**5:30 p.m.** Charmers shouted obscenities at women at 15th and H streets. They denied it.

**5:57 – 6:09 p.m.** Alleged drunks were scraped off the Schwazz and Pink-plopped for a therapeutic ignominy wallow.

• **Thursday, July 5 12:37 a.m.** Two parties on Sunset Avenue overlapped, merged, coalesced and metastasized into a 300-400 person blowout. Two highly beveraged chaps wound up in jail.

**1:05 p.m.** Several kittens found tied to the bumper of a van at Ninth and H streets were scooped up by the Animal Control officer, who now, officially, has seen everything.

**1:56 p.m.** No license or registration, but more than enough stickybud – apparently *not* issued by the DMV – at 11th and J streets, and a Eureka man enjoyed county lodging.

**6:28 p.m.** A gender-indeterminate individuloid in a red gown loomed near a Valley West coffee outlet for a bit.

**8:28 p.m.** Someone alleged all kindsa *bad, bad* things going on at Ninth and H, but that turned out not to be the case.

**11:35 – 11:59 p.m.** If you wanted to attract police scrutiny – and who doesn't? – one proven technique would be to allegedly toss objects at passersby from your car, then linger in the area. An under-21er implemented this methodology and was cited and released for allegedly transporting alcohol and having a blood alky level higher than .01 percent.

• **Friday, July 6 11:41 a.m.** Marijuana-muddled travelers had a forgettable encounter with an officer in the 900 block of F Street, and that should be easy for them. One was jailed, one released.

**1:14 – 2:02 p.m.** Sometimes it just seems that life is one great big argument.

**3:08 p.m.** One youth allegedly pursued the short route to loserhood by packing alcohol and cigarettes.

• **Saturday, July 7 7:08 a.m.** A crumpled heap of a man on Old Arcata Road told police he was fine, appearances notwithstanding.

**4:16 p.m.** A loud household argument on Virginia Way was more or less typical of the breed.

**4:40 p.m.** Another ripoff at an I Street cooperative supermarket.

**7:50 – 9:13 p.m.** The 1800 block of Blakeslee Avenue was a troubled place this night. First a plant was stolen from in front of a woman's home, and then, a dog barked more than necessary.

• **Monday, July 9 12:01 a.m.** Move to Arcata with your menagerie-in-a-motor home, they told her in Shasta County – Humboldt people will surely understand your *incredible empathy* for animals and drop everything to lavish scarce public services on you and your critter club. But whatever their motives, her travel advisors' characterization of Humboldt's indulgence proved overly generous. Contacted in the 1100 block of Fifth Street.

**1:21 a.m.** A Eurekan and a McKinleyviller met halfway – in Arcata, to argue outside a G Street restaurant.

**9:25 a.m.** A campout at the Ball Park – now *there's* a good idea.

**3:05 p.m.** Those prank calls are getting old.

**3:50 p.m.** It's *my* kitten. No, it's *mine*. And so on between two women in the 500 block of Ninth Street until police waded in. One woman left with the disputed feline.

**6:45 p.m.** A traveler wasn't sufficiently mellowed by his alleged pot stash to avoid an assault charge in the 700 block of Eighth Street and a ride to the Pink House.

**7:31 p.m.** A woman's bike disappeared from her F Street home. For you and I, just another little coplog item. For her, major suckage.

**10:45 p.m.** Annoying phone calls between exes carry that special aroma of desperation.

**• Wednesday, July 11 7:07 a.m.**
Three travelers passing through town
In Redwood Park ran, like, aground
Illegally campin'
Till cops somewhat dampened
The prospect of hanging around.

**8:39 p.m.** Sixth and H really wants to be a quiet residential neighb, and once was, but now, between the dragsters on the street and the shrieking drunks on the sidewalk, periods of silence are all too fleeting.

**• Thursday, July 12 9 p.m.** The theory is, a piece of paper can make an unreasonable person at least stay away.

**3:23 p.m.** Another restraining order was hopefully deployed.

**• Friday, July 13 5:45 a.m.**
In Redwood Park campers played house
Which makes Redwood regulars grouse
As day was aborning
A cop gave a warning
To locate more legal redoubts.

**10:43 p.m.**
A barking dog on Heather Lane
Emitted arfs that drilled the brain
Of someone who called in the cops
By then the dog had shut its chops.

**• Saturday, July 14 11:54 – 11:57 a.m.** Good arguing weather at Seventh and K streets and at the D Street Neighborhood Center.

**1:53 p.m.** Doke smopers puffed and stumbled dazedly from Redwood Park.

**9 p.m.** Someone verbally aggressed the guy with the Help Me sign and dogs at 17th and G streets, an act as pointless as it is unwarranted.

**• Sunday, July 15 9:21 p.m.** If they made a pulp novel of this incident, it might be named *Pot, Booze, Gasoline and Steel Bars.*

**• Monday, July 16 8:26 a.m.** That building has to have layers of paint as thick as the walls underneath at this point, after the latest graffiti-coverup – a lengthy hip hop-derived screed temporarily immortalized in Krylon – at Sunny Brae's present-day palimpsest.

**1:22 p.m.** It cannot be confirmed that the subjects in full bicker at the car wash sported mullet hairstyles, but it seems awfully likely.

**4:30 p.m.** The paperwork necessary to obtain a restraining order can be as onerous as the nimrod who's on your case. If every box isn't checked, it's all for nothing.

**6:22 p.m.** Skateboarding on the roof of the decrepit post-industrial ruins on South I Street surely earned one adolescent daredevil his anti-merit badge.

**5:27 p.m.** Tensile failure in the 2300 block of Baldwin Street, and the cable guy made some overtime.

**6:46 p.m.** Oh man, that was one big mixup at the trailer park.

**7:31 p.m.** South G has its moments, too.

**8:54 p.m.** A "transient" who wanders among us all year 'round was arrested on charges of theft and possession of a drug needle at an I Street cooperative supermarket. *Priorities,* man.

**• Thursday, July 19 1:28 a.m.** First, alleged beastliness wore out a Blue Laker's welcome at a Valley West budget motel.

**2:24 a.m.** Then, a donut shop denizen was deemed unfit to share the premises with fluorescent-tanned maple bars.

**5:05 p.m.** An officer attempted contact with a man found sleeping at the Redwood Lodge. But the startled subject fled, his dreads and facial mane bouncing in the breeze as he bounded into the woods.

**11:58 p.m.** Too young, with an I.D. too fake and on probation anyway, a youth was arrested outside a Tavern Row social establishment and caged.

**• Friday, July 20 5:35 a.m.** Where do they go, those car campers awakened at this hour? Somewhere else.

**10:41 a.m.** There was this big argument in Redwood Park over who owned the dog. A veterinarian offered definitive information and the dog escaped halving.

**9:57 p.m.** An "electric fence" was reported bordering the south side of Stewart Park. The property owner, an amateur photographer, was apprised of Section 8033 of the Arcata Municipal Code, which states in part that: "Fences charged to any voltage shall not be allowed in any City areas except those zoned for agricultural use..." But there's little ag use of the park other than hearty harvests of resentment, the fence wasn't really electric – more of a symbolic gift to humanity – and in any case it was reduced to a pile of phony electric fence stuff by the middle of last week.

• **Saturday, July 21 1:47–2:11 a.m.** Marsh amenities include a public phone with which disenfranchised theoretical physicists may make bogus 911 calls.

**5:44 a.m.** For not the first time, he stood by dolefully as an officer authored another citation for him to autograph. This time, it was all about camping and outstanding warrants, out at the Marsh.

**6:12 a.m.** It's as if they're breeding illegal Redwood Park campers somewhere.

**3:35 p.m.** A semi-pro baseball team coach reported a player refusing to leave the Ball Park. An officer pitched some reality and the player left.

**7:23 p.m.** A dog was reported trying to jump out of the window of the Chico woman's mobile kennel/residence at 14th and H streets. It's a big Ford with a shell, full of dogs and living here and there around town as its sketchy transmission permits. A cop spoke, she listened and rumbled away, and what, really, changed?

**8:39 p.m.** Hopefully, the fellow who was Pinked after being caught in the 1100 block of I Street while allegedly under the influence of a controlled sub while driving, doing so with a suspended license and probation violation isn't typical of the menfolk of Yuba City.

**11:20 p.m.** A family business trying to move from the action-packed Plaza to a new location at Seventh and G streets has had its new building bothered, battered and busted up even before construction is complete. Knocked-down construction fences and smashed windows aren't propitious portents for the future, and the owner – a genuine craftsman in an age of disposable, mass-produced shoddiness – is already talking McKinleyville.

• **Sunday, July 22 5:52 a.m.** An unknown, self-appointed Public Works activist without portfolio (or brains) removed a sewer hole cover between 16th and I streets for reasons unfathomable.

**8:36 p.m.** A representative of the non-cost-effective gender was seen dangling his pale, hairy legs over the northeast Giuntoli Lane overpass. The fate-tempter was gone on police arrival.

• **Thursday, August 9 2:20 a.m.** Three galoots, abdomens bulging and arteries coursing with cholesterol-laden delights, did a scarf-'n'-scram at a Janes Road pattern restaurant.

**3:55 a.m.** A traveler bunked down amid the graffiti and spittle at the surreally contoured Skate Park until asked to leave.

• **Friday, August 10 9:07 a.m.** A trio of nicotine hobbyists blithely engulfed McKinley's overcoat hem in a sour bluish miasma of lung exhaust.

• **Saturday, August 11 12:54 a.m.** A man caterwauling insensibly near a Northtown motel was arrested on the pedestrian footbridge on a charge of bein' all likkered up.

**8:10 a.m.** A coupla folks chugged up the grueling hill towards Redwood Park, the wheels of the shopping cart they'd commandeered objecting noisily to the uphill journey. An officer persuaded them to return the ungainly stainless steel affair.

**11:24 a.m.** The camping woman with her half-dozen big dogs had all her stuff piled up in an F Street laundromat's parking lot while she cleaned out the camper/kennel, triggering a complaint by the laundro's manager. When an Animal Control officer greeted her, she explained that gee, she's spent a lot of time in this lot and no one complained before. But that gemlike logic held little persuasion, and she agreed to move along following the methodical turdectomy.

• **Monday, August 13 1:20 p.m.** A motion sensor was stolen from the men's bathroom at the Redwood Lodge on the 11th Street side of Redwood Park. Don't worry, you bought another one for something over $100.

**2:24 p.m.** Yo, dude – cranial trauma ain't really as much fun as it sounds. Put on a helmet and pads.

**7:10 p.m.** A traveler was arrested on a trespassing charge at a never-a-dull-moment I Street cooperative supermarket, and went to the always-a-dull-evening Pink House.

• **Tuesday, August 14 1:06–2 a.m.** Apparently it's true what they say about back alleys late at night.

**8:26 a.m.** A tailgate was reported stolen from a vehicle on Charles Avenue.

• **Tuesday, August 14 12:05 p.m.** A goon in a maroon Ford Taurus with a touch-o'-class broken left tailight drove aggro-style and made gang-style hand signs at someone near 10th and H streets.

• **Wednesday, August 15 2:35 a.m.** The world's most low-effort, but also short-lived campsite – a doorway at Ninth and H streets – hosted a citizen-government encounter. Soon both were gone.

**5:59 p.m.** An H Street Plaza business complained of an unspecified number of persons clumped up outside on the narrow sidewalk. Advised of the complaint, the squattage dissipated to more rumpworthy realms.

• **Thursday, August 16 7:47 p.m.** A visitor from Palm Springs lost a wallet and its contents to an agent of evil in the 600 block of F Street.

**10:49 p.m.** Hopefully, that reckless driver at 11th Street and Janes Road will hurt only him/herself when the statistical imperative finally asserts itself.

• **Friday, August 17 12:51 a.m.** Someone reported a major kablooey in the 800 block of Chapman Court, but someone else said it was just a firecracker.

**11:45 a.m.** A Eureka guy's unguarded food stamps lasted about four nanoseconds in Redwood Park.

**12:05 p.m.** Unleashed dogs ran-'n'-shat on the 11th Street side of Redwood Park, near the playgrounds. An officer talked with dog owners while the feces glistened and fumed in the noonday sun, awaiting the inevitable footfall.

**3:56 p.m.** A McKinleyville representative was arrested at fabled Ninth and H streets on charges of packing and pitching a controlled sub. Off to the county cage.

• **Saturday, August 18 1:32 – 2:46 a.m.** It's impossible to find a decent Huckle-Buff these days, though more contemporary adult beverages consumed to excess and regurgitated downtown will do nicely. Booked and lodged.

**2:15 p.m.** A yard sale encroached on pedestrian rights-of-way at 12th and F Streets. Bric-a-brac was retracted.

**8:06 p.m.** Humans convincingly mimicked baboon behaviors in the 900 block of G Street. Fortunately, at least one had a functioning limbic system.

**8:25 p.m.** The periphery of a dry, heavily wooded redwood forest in the dryest days of summer – a perfect time to touch off a big bonfire in Redwood Park. Some disaster-flirters were counseled.

• **Sunday, August 19 1:26 a.m.** Young and drunk in the sour fluorescent light of a 24-hour eatery's parking lot, making a lot of noise in the middle of the night... these are memories to last a lifetime.

**2:43 a.m.** A brace of youths were said to be randomly attacking people in the 1000 block of H Street. Three putative punks were snagged on assault and battery charges, one also being charged with driving in a post-cocktail scenario. Mommies and daddies converged on APD headquarters.

**9:51 a.m.** A genius dumped garbage, including mail with his name on it, on someone's Eastern Avenue property. Wait'll Mensa finds out.

**6:13 p.m.** A youth was arrested on charges of funny ID and unfunny corruption of a minor near Redwood Park. A traveler journeyed to the Pink House.

• **Monday, August 20 12:50 a.m.** Neighbors felt the pain of a neighbor – or heard it anyway – as he bellowed obscenities in the 1800 block of Blakeslee Avenue.

**5:02 p.m.** Little did the four travelers at the former lumber mill in the 1200 block of Fifth Street realize their hardscrabble soiree was taking place atop a spreading plume of one of the most potent carcinogens this side of plutonium – pentachlorophenol, known in its glory days as Woodlife, a wholesome-sounding, miraculously effective fungicide which was liberally slathered on milled lumber and dumped on the ground all over town. The contamination is presently being remediated at the site, which may or may not work, but in the meantime stay away from the blackberries and.. *what?* You already *ate...* Oh well, have a nice day, chaps.

**7:27 p.m.** Roommates fell out, and re-enacted the timeless tussle over what belonged to whom.

**9:16 p.m.** It wouldn't be an Arcata evening without an uncontrolled dog lunging at people downtown.

• **Tuesday, August 21 1:58 a.m.** Sixth and H is like some kind of howling-permissible zone, except that it's not. A loudie agreed to vociferate at diminished amplitude.

**6:19 a.m.** A half-dozen free spirits asnooze in Redwood Park awoke to a cordial but businesslike greeting by a City emissary. One wasn't who he said he was, and tried out a plank-like bunk in the Pink House.

• **Wednesday, August 22 1:30 a.m.** If you had an upstairs office on the Plaza and worked late, you'd take to the roof for a breather every so often, too.

**9:01 a.m.** *Amen, not albumen!* A Hallen Drive spiritual worship facility was egg-besplatterated.

**10:51 a.m.** With the 14th Street parking lot of Redwood Park serving as a sort of base camp for travelers and their omnipresent dogs this summer, it was only a matter of time until a full-on horseshoe pit was erected in the area, this one appearing beside Trail 1. Two four-inch diameter logs were jammed in the ground perhaps 30 feet apart, with an interlocking, "log cabin"-style backing erected. Conversion of the natural area to a mini-sporting arena took an inevitable toll, with local vegetation wiped out. A City forest tech uprooted the installation and began clearing up the trash and scattered refuse against a backdrop of jeers from idlers lounging in the area, who offered no assistance. "We care about the forest," they declared, appearances notwithstanding.

**12:31 – 12:43 p.m.** Dogs, dogs, dogs, loose in Redwood Park.

**3:38 p.m.** Some people just don't like a stranger staring hungrily at them and asking for money as they do ATM business.

**4:12 p.m.** This picnic-filled park is just perfect – for my dog to run wild in!

**8:34 p.m.** Redwood Park again went to the dogs, though on police arrival the romping pets perhaps coincidentally were suddenly restrained.

• **Thursday, August 23 3:07 a.m.** Stewart Park's weird juju blossomed again, with a group of folks reported doing who-knows-what to the sprinklers. Turned out they were just playing in the water. At 3 a.m. "There were a lot of drunk kids running around, and we were playing with the sprinklers and stuff," said an 18-year-old participant, still in touch with his inner child. "We were just having fun."

**8:06 a.m.** A driver fled from an officer on Spear Avenue, with the vehicle later found in Valley West. It had been stolen in Westhaven.

**9:45 a.m.** If enough people did what this traveler is accused of, there wouldn't even *be* an I Street cooperative supermarket.

**12:21 p.m.** A tobacco enthusiast indulged in his avocation at Ninth and H until warned that we just don't do that kind of thing around there.

**2:05 p.m.** A Plaza business hired a new general manager from out of the area, who worked one day and disappeared.

The AWOL manager was tracked down in Idaho a week later, and said that a family matter there had suddenly required her presence. "No call, nothing, zero," said an employee.

• **Friday, August 24 11:49 a.m.** If the sour smoke was somehow immediately absorbed by the cigarette user's eyebrows or something, and if the butt just evaporated away into nothingness, it wouldn't matter if someone lit up on the Plaza. But besides mucking up the place for others, smoking there remains a dandy way to draw cops, then get arrested on charges of marijuana possession and an old but still spry arrest warrant, and Pink Housed.

• **Saturday, August 25 10:54 a.m.** A traveler plopped down on the Ninth and H sidewalk and turned his dog loose – just a little something he does for the rest of us.

**11:24 a.m.** There's lots of handy things to tie a dog to at the Farmers' Market, where, for health reasons, dogs are prohibited. A Eureka woman was cited.

**1:21 p.m.** A woman on the Plaza offered police a serviceable if inspecific tale involving her giving money to some guy she didn't know who was going to "rent a piece of property to her," but now he was nowhere to be found, and the failsafe business arrangement collapsed.

**2:44 p.m.** Reports that a nine-foot-tall bronze figure of a dead president came to life on the Plaza, staggered over and smashed that blaring boom box on the north side are, unfortunately, idle fantasy.

• **Sunday, August 26 2:03–2:28 a.m.** Glug, clink, slam.

**3:36 a.m.** A driver's license, sobriety... those are for *other* people. Jail – that's for me!

**7:54 a.m.** Dogs went arf-happy on Golf Course Road at an hour some neighbors little suspected even existed.

• **Tuesday, August 28 1:47 a.m.** Quick as a wink, you're in the Pink – *House*, that is, thanks to Inepto-Dismol, allegedly comprised of dueling doses of marijuana and alcohol.

**11:45 a.m.** A woman asked police how the government could help keep that guy away from her.

**12:12 p.m.** Dude packin' an Oh-Zee at the ITF, said APD.

• **Wednesday, August 29 6:36 p.m.** If what they say is true, this traveler was something of a one-person party at Ninth and H streets – drinkin', drunken, packin' smoke and breakin' probation, none of which was possible at his subsequent locale – the Pink House.

**8:08 p.m.** A fella got all excited at Ninth and H.

• **Thursday, August 30 12:20 a.m.** An ill-fated foray into an entirely too well-lit 24-hour supermarket on F Street ended with an arrest, a shoplifing charge and confiscation of an unspecified dope-fiend device.

**12:34 p.m.** The entrance to the Ball Park is not the enchanted drug-ingestion grotto some people keep trying to make it.

**Late report** Alcohol isn't doing this guy or his breath any good.

**10:39 p.m.**
A Ninth and H travelin' type
So out was allegedly wiped
He huffed and he puffed
Until collared and cuffed
And Pinked on a drunkenness gripe.

**11:12 – 11:50 p.m.** Anyone who complains about loud noise, whether on Susan Street, D Street or upper G Street, just doesn't understand the parity relationship between amplitude and jollity. Things settled down after a while.

• **Friday, August 31 2:03 a.m.** August 31 not being any particularly festive holiday, it's hard to understand why anyone on probation would get behind the wheel drunk and toting pot, as police allege.

**1:22 p.m.** A traveler allegedly forgot the paying-for-it part at an I Street cooperative supermarket.

**1:25 p.m.** Cutting one of life's little corners by dumping your household trash in someone else's dumpster actually doubles the nuisance value of the whole undertaking when you hafta go back and get it under the judgmental glare of the legal dumpstermeister.

**5:43 p.m.** Another welcome-to-my-dog incident in Redwood Park.

**9:47 p.m.** An Oasis Street hissy-spat ended in a Pink House stay for an allegedly cocktail-reeled woman.

• **Saturday, September 1 1:53 a.m.** They who wander parking lots late at night howling low-bit communications at each other – these in the 1900 block of H Street – are bound to get official attention.

**4:43 p.m.** A guy got on a City bus and found out that it didn't go to Eureka, which clashed unexpectedly with his reality paradigm. Naturally, he blamed the driver, got snotty and bailed.

• **Sunday, September 2 2:51 p.m.** Roberts Court East residents unleashed their dogs on the world until warned about the Municipal Code violation and abrogation of simple common sense.

**8:38 p.m.** Another lost soul was reported staggering in and out of the roadway on Samoa Boulevard east of the train tracks. It wandered away.

**9:59 p.m.**
In parking lots conflicts go down
When family membs have a showdown
Mom/daughter co-yelled
Near a V-West motel
In a vituperation hoedown.

• **Monday, September 3 3:23 a.m.** And yet another incident of arfs obtruding on what's supposed to be the dead o' night.

**11:24 a.m.** No, you aren't the one person who's allowed to bring your dog onto the Plaza.

**12:52 – 1:11 p.m.** You'd think the timeless beauty of majestic Redwood Park would be mood-enhancer enough. But not, allegedly, for these two.

• **Tuesday, September 4 5:55 p.m.** They call it the Intermodal Transit Facility – an ungainly moniker matched in awkwardness only by the dunderheaded design of the place, where bicycles, lockers for holding valuables and telephones are placed as far away from view of on-site personnel as possible. This is a big help to thieves, who routinely undermine the theory of the facility being a multi-mode transportation hub by stealing, vandalizing and rendering inoperative people's vehicles and the ever-diminishing amenities there. And even if you could read the time on the clock with the needle-like hands without squinting, it's often inaccurate and completely misleading in determining when the next bus is coming. Meanwhile, one commuter would like his bike back.

• **Wednesday, September 5 2:38 p.m.** Someone thought they saw a weirdo at Ninth and H.

**3:29 p.m.** It's just that when you skateboard on the sidewalk, people can't walk there, my fine young dunce. Oh, and it's illegal, too.

• **Thursday, September 6 2:40 a.m.** Those two travelers didn't have much to say, but they said it loud enough for multiple residents in the area of 10th and N streets to phone police. Advised of the complaints, the twosome toddled.

**8:12 a.m.** That truck camper who loves animals more than the rest of us will ever understand left her dogs locked up in her truck at 12th and D streets while she went off to further her interest in ceramics. The canned canines had adequate ventilation, water and food, so why do they howl so pitifully?

**9:57 a.m.** With one missing and the others mercilessly molested, an 11th Street business will henceforth keep its potted plants indoors during non-biz hours.

**1:43-3:04 p.m.** Dope in the forest and the streets, ripoffs in the stores, vandals on someone's fence, a car burgled. Mayberry this ain't.

• **Friday, September 7 12:21 a.m.** A skulker was reported fussing in the no-man's-land alley behind a Valley West liquor store. A traveler said he was just looking for his dog... yeah, that's it, looking for his dog.

**1:58 a.m.** *Note to self:* when on probation, drunk and without a driver's license, flashing a fake-o I.D. at a cop may not be a career move.

**7:41 a.m.** One traveler shouted with another on the desolate garbagescape known as the 14th Street Redwood Park parking lot.

**3:44 p.m.** The person who ripped off that heartful little H Street clothing shop now has some really nice duds and an eternity under the merciless dominion of Beelzebub.

• **Saturday, September 8 12:18 a.m.** One man's ceiling is another man's floor in the 600 block of 14th Street.

**1:23-2:44 a.m.** The ranks of the Pink House swelled with a number of booze-woozed souls.

**1:32 p.m.** Ranger Bob was the last guy an alleged Redwood Park marijuana aficionado wanted to meet up with.

• **Sunday, September 9 11:28 p.m.** A South H Street res found a shopping cart fulla some guy's stuff outside her home. A trav gathered his meagers and shambled away.

• **Monday, September 10 11:25 a.m.**
Two travelers, Peter and Ray
Allegedly sought to purvey
Some pot in the park
But too quick to say "nark!"
Ranger Bob came and ruined their day.

**2:11 p.m.** That traveler may not have had a Co-op number, but it had his. He was arrested on a burglary charge and Pinked.

**9:52 p.m.** Two unwashed types who, with eyes darting, slumped self-consciously around a downtown office building, packing what appeared to be their worldly possessions in bulging backpacks and calling the working people there "bro," were clearly out of place and took their leave.

• **Tuesday, September 11 1:13 p.m.** Following a season of warm, sunny days, Arcata's weather synchronized with the sudden plummet in the national mood as a coarse, wind-whipped drizzle pelted a gloomy downtown. At Ninth and H, two travelers were rounded up on probation violation charges and a warrant. As officers tucked the two into a cruiser, free-range cretins circled, jabbering vile abuse at the cops. *"Whyncha go ketch some terrorists, myaaan?"* was one standarounder's helpful catcall.

• **Thursday, September 13 9:31 a.m.** Someone was

supposedly firing a cannon into the forest from East 14th Street, but police found no one home.

**10:11 a.m.** Two saggy-clad folk got into a shouty showdown out front of the post office. Cops came with flashers on and sirens blaring, only to find fragmented melon remnants and the saggies scuttling purposefully away. They were I.D.'d, said they were fine, and that was that.

• **Friday, September 14 12:14 a.m.** Midnight-hour elegance knows no better definition than a scuffle in a mini-mart parking lot.

**1:29 a.m.** A Riversider ran drunkenly aground in the Tavern Row's butt-end alley, said police. A nauseating ride on a sticky, puke-scented vinyl seat to a loud, clangy, hard place. Hands bound behind, his eyes squinted in pain at the fluorescent glare, slowly adjusting to take in an institutional nightmare world gone insanely... *Pink?*

**5:47 a.m.** Travelers Ken, Tara and Geoff bunked down on South I streets, but arose probably earlier than planned.

**12:40-2:26 p.m.** Maybe it's the marijuana that lets those who hang out and trash the once-pleasant 14th Street Redwood Park lot feel OK about what the place has become. A clutch of clueless cannabinators were Ranger Bobbed.

• **Saturday, September 15 1:15 a.m.** Drunk in public, probation violation and outstanding warrants, all in one handy two-legged Pinkable package at Ninth and H.

**3:15 p.m.** *Allegedly...*
A quartet of cannabinoid users
Attuned to elude cops in cruisers
Met nice Ranger Bob
Whose interesting job
Includes busting Redwood Park schmoozers

**9:47 p.m.** Menfolk exercised the specialty of their gender, thumping chests at Ninth and H.

• **Monday, September 17 12:05 p.m.** An aggresive dog at Vaissade Park was taken to the City Pound by Animal Control, a one-man force charged with cleaning up other peoples' irresponsibilities toward living beings.

**1:03 p.m.** Why do normal people eschew the Intermodal Transient Facility as a useable transportation node? This guy might be one reason. Booked and lodged.

**8:10 p.m.** Another trav was found with pot on the Plaza, which triggered background checks. Ka-*ching!* Outstanding warrants, jail...

• **Tuesday, September 18 7:27 a.m.** A loosed steed frolicked and pranced through Bayside. Animal Control rounded up the horsie and returned it to its owner.

• **Wednesday, September 19 2:56 a.m.** The Oasis Street debating society went nuclear again...

**4:47 a.m.** ...with hostilities continuing into the weeest of hours.

**10:10 a.m.** A traveler was reported camping on South F Street, but wasn't found until...

**10:50 a.m.** ... he was reported following people into a storage facility when they opened the gate. He was warned about this, that and the other thing.

**11:50 a.m.** If you thought that big backlog of traffic tickets and the registered letter from the cops was just too much trouble to deal with, imagine the sudden setback factor pursuant to finding an immobilizing metal device booted onto your rear wheel.

**12:42 p.m.**
Beneath Big Bill's bronze-alloy flankies
Two trav'lers got fussy and cranky
Till Robocop landed
And then they disbanded
To fresh exploits equally swanky.

**1:17 p.m.** One minute you're taking a dump behind the 600 block of J Street, and the next you're at the receiving end of a ticket being written by a bike cop who whooshed onto the scene altogether too fast. Life's like that.

**3:57 p.m.** A travelers alleged illegal pharmacopeia yielded to official scrutiny, and was confiscated by the stealthily wheeled officer. Pot, 'shrooms, and off to Big Pink.

**• Thursday, September 20 2:33 a.m.** A Plaza toy store lost its front window to unknown glass-haters.

**8:21 a.m.**
A traveler, aimless and haggard
In Giuntoli Lane traffic staggered
Police caught his eye
At an onramp nearby
And bade farewell to the lost laggard.

**12:12 p.m.** There's little else to do in an alley behind the 1000 block of G Street but argue over nothing much.

**12:47 p.m.** A traveler's alleged smokeables were placed impossibly far away from his beckoning lungs at the Intermodal Transient Facility.

**5:29 p.m.** Buncha paint spilled on Samoa Boulevard. Orange-clad cleanup forces, their imaginations fired by visions of overtime checks, descended on the splatter site.

## IMBROGLIO EXTRA

# HELEN WILSON'S
# ANIMAL
# ARCATA

**A**rcata is known for diversity amongst its people. But it's not just the people that add character to the town. The animals in the area have a story as well, and sometimes, when people and critters collide, adventures happen.

Arcata's animals come from many different backgrounds. There's the unusual pets that the college students bring to the area, the wild animals that roam in and around the forest and, of course, the domestic pet that witnesses it all.

In Arcata, the days of the "Dog Catcher" seem to be over, as severe budget cuts have curtailed what we now know as "Animal Control." Even so, human/ animal encounters continue, from bears to mountain lions, ferrets to seals and a

**Nick Albert in his element.**

loose boa constrictor every now and then. Loss of the Animal Control officer has given Arcata Police another layer of responsibility, which sometimes takes them from fighting crime to locating a bear roaming the City or an elk in someone's backyard.

Nick Albert, patrol captain of the Department of Fish and Game, has many stories to tell of the animals that have left a lasting impression on him. He moved from San Francisco in 1977 and has been working in fields involving animal control issues ever since.

During Albert's first days in Arcata he visited the Plaza and walked down the sidewalk where Arcata Stationers is located today. He felt something looking at him over his shoulder and turned to see a mountain lion in the back of a man's pick-up truck. "It scared the pants off me," he stated, laughing. The lion was tied to the truck with a chain around its neck. Upon investigation, Albert found that the lion had been in an elderly man's possession since before it became illegal to own a mountain lion, so he was able to keep it. Albert and other Arcata citizens saw the man frequently around town, always toting his friendly pet mountain lion with him.

Albert recalls another story about a bull elk living in a yard on B and 11th streets. The elk was very comfortable spending its days by a small creek on the property. Albert was shocked to find out that the elk had been living there for over a month, but the owner of the property assured him that the elk was not causing a problem and was welcome to stay.

Eventually the elk moved further down the creek to some cow pastures located behind a California Highway Patrol office and began grazing with the cows. This was fine for a while, and the ranchers didn't see a problem with it, but then breeding season began and the inevitable happened.

The bull elk gathered the cows together and took possession of them, just as elk do with other elk during breeding season. It became very protective of the cows and was aggressive when the ranchers came near to brand or care for them. The ranchers became upset and

**An elk among the bovines near Samoa Boulevard.**

asked for help in having the antlered interloper removed.

The elk was tranquilized, put in a livestock trailer and a tag was placed on his ear. Then he was taken to forest service lands and monitored closely. Authorities looked on as he quickly and happily reunited with other elk.

All departments that come in contact with animal issues in Arcata, including the fire department, the police department and the Fish and Game department, tell stories of animals ending up in unusual places. Susan Chase of APD tells of a phone call that she received about a lizard being found in the Sunny Brae area of Arcata. A trash can had been placed over it to prevent it from escaping before authorities arrived. When officers showed up they found that the "lizard" under the trash can was a Gila monster, a poisonous kind of lizard that is illegal in California.

According to Albert, it's rare that bears or mountain lions are found west of U.S. Highway 101, which runs through town. However, there are exceptions. Several years ago, on a Friday or Saturday night, police received a call around 9 p.m. about a bear in the dumpster area of the Arcata Safeway store. The bear was gone by the time police arrived. Throughout the night police received call after call from residents who had spotted the bear, and they tracked its slow movement through town.

The bear visited many places that night, but avoided

the Plaza area. Eventually it returned to where it was first spotted, the Safeway parking lot, and was never seen again. Albert says that animals usually end up in town when they are lost and confused. If they are healthy they will return to their natural environment as soon as they are able.

Another time, a bear was reported on the eastern side of the bottom of Fickle Hill Road. The bear was observed sitting on his rear in the middle of a vegetable garden, snacking on veggies. The bear didn't seem to mind that a group of police officers were trying to scare him out of the yard, and it continued munching on the greens. Luckily the department's veterinarian was in town and she managed to tranquilize the animal.

After the bear was sedated, it had to be moved away from the City. It was blindfolded, and its paws were tied with a hobble, a device that acts as handcuffs for animals. It took four men to lift the bear into the truck that would take it to Eureka, where it would be

**As if cats, dogs, opossums, bears, mountain lions and ferrets aren't enough to deal with, even sea otters make an occasional appearance at Arcata's Marsh & Wildlife Sanctuary.**

transferred to a culvert trap.

The bear was supposed to remain sedated for this procedure, but when the truck was opened, the bear, without hobbles or a blindfold, ran out of the truck and behind the Eureka office. Officers then underwent the task of re-sedating the bear and finally managed to return him to the forest.

History has proven that where college students live, there's bound to be an odd or illegal pet or two. And with Humboldt State University nestled in the city, Arcata is home to a lot of students. Many of the pets that students shelter are ignored, as they are mostly well cared for and don't cause a problem. But sometimes these animals are dangerous, and in the wrong hands, can cause problems for many people. Students have been found possessing iguanas, boa constrictors, pythons and an assortment of other exotic critters. Tales abound of animals escaping and needing to be captured, often with the owner's help. One student found that his large boa constrictor had gone missing. The snake had made its way around a neighborhood and scared several people. Authorities had been called and were trying to coax the snake into a duffel bag when the student arrived to help remedy the situation.

Another student, or recent graduate, was advertising the sale of the illegal, beautiful and rare Gila monsters. Police responded by sending an undercover officer to the apartment to buy one of the "lizards." Upon arrival the officer found not only the Gila monsters, but copperhead snakes and other poisonous reptiles for sale as well. The student also owned a vicious crocodile that was kept in a large plastic tub and a five-foot docile alligator in the bathtub, which he claimed to have raised since it was a juvenile. The student was cited for a misdemeanor, and some of the animals were removed from his possession. According to Albert, animals are often moved out of California to states where they are legal. This is preferred over destroying the animal, although sometimes animals have to be destroyed.

Ferrets – always popular with college students – raise a smile and a rueful shake of the head from Albert. He appears torn between affection for the endearing little weasels and his duty to enfore Fish & Game's staunch, decades-old anti-ferret statutes.

Sometimes people do more harm than good when they try to care for animals. Raccoons can be aggressive and leave a mess of trash and other debris in their path, so when police received a complaint about them being fed in a Sunny Brae neighborhood, they tried to get the family to stop the activity. The population of raccoons in Sunny Brae increased, but the family would not stop the daily feedings. It wasn't until mountain lions were drawn to the area and began feeding on the raccoons that the family realized their mistake. The raccoons left the area after they stopped receiving handouts, and they took the mountain lions with them.

From bears to mountain lions to ferrets to seals, Arcata has lots of animals. Usually animals and people mix well and can happily share a town, but sometimes problems arise and authorities need to be called. When this happens, the support and help that the people of the town provide shows the true spirit of the area. Arcata's abundance and diversity of animal life, wild and companionable, helps makes it and its law enforcement challenges unique. *– H.W.*

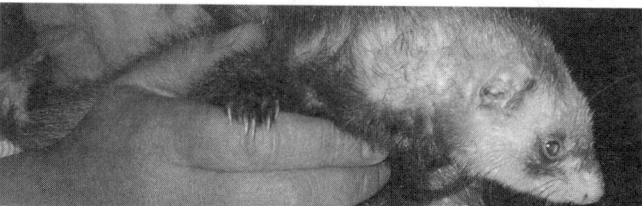

**Ferret fugitive Bonnie at an undisclosed Arcata location.**

**5:31 p.m.** Setting a backpack down on an Arcata street is like placing a treasure chest full of diamonds and rubies and crystal chalices and stuff like that near a bunch of pirates. A street buccaneer snagged the hapless knapsack.

**11:09 p.m.** Derrick and Geoff became entangled in a huff-and-bicker spiral from which there was no face-saving escape other than uniformed intervention.

• **Friday, September 21 3:19 p.m.** A nomadic napper unreeled a sleeping bag on the Plaza for a little camp-out. The folly was short-lived.

**4:15 p.m.** After allegedly mouthing off to dark-skinned folk at 15th and G, a 19-year-old self-styled superpatriot was arrested and jailed on hate crime charges.

**5:50 p.m.** Once the car battery was recharged, a driver zoomed away from a downtown service station, paying in Karma rather than cash.

• **Monday, October 1 7:33 a.m.** A "space box" was reported stolen from a vehicle in Valley West.

**8:31 a.m.** The sonic output emanating from Apartment 2 came in the worst possible combination: a "loud stereo with bad music." An officer pounded on the door to no avail, and went back to the station to see if the bad music aficionado would notice his phone ringing. No word on the outcome.

**1:09 p.m.** Next time she buys a bike, she'll probably invest in a "college town"-rated lock.

• **Tuesday, October 2 3:21 p.m.** Sometimes people think they have territorial dominion over parking on the street in front of their homes.

**3:41 p.m.** He wanted money, and told I Street passersby in no uncertain terms. Police paid a call.

**4:20 p.m.** What foolishness to leave anything stealable attached to one's bike at the Intermodal Transient Facility.

**9:01 p.m.** A traveler hit emotional bottom in the 100 block of 14th Street when his vehicle became disabled. "Oh, *God,*" he implored an uncaring automotive deity. All an officer had by way of spiritual advice was information on the City camping ordinance.

• **Wednesday, October 3 12:36 p.m.** Like a measly chain can stop today's brave new bike thief on L.K. Wood Boulevard?

• **Thursday, October 4 7:49 p.m.** Two subscribers to the hairy-beardo-baggy pants fashion statement boosted a bottle of Southern Comfort from an F Street supermarket.

• **Saturday, October 6 12:54 a.m.** He was sound asleep when his dad woke him up asking for a cigarette lighter. An argument ensued, police came and the dad 'n' lad lighter-fighters were separated for the night.

• **Sunday, October 7 2:51 a.m.** Another drunk bites the dust on the Plaza.

**4:10 a.m.** Imagine having to call the police over your very roommate's stereo. An officer conversed with noise-boy through his bedroom window, brokering a shaky peace.

**4 p.m.** Loose dogs and even looser drinkers infested the 11th Street/playground side of Redwood Park.

**10:08 p.m.** A Spear Avenue resident reported a male-type human in his backyard performing the specialty of the breed – stumbling around and cursing. The interloper without portfolio meandered away in a random direction.

• **Tuesday, October 9 9:17 a.m.** What towering illogic, what overarching cluelessness, what fantastical construct of utter self-delusion led a camera owner to place a shiny object on a Plaza bench and expect it to remain unmolested for more than, say, a second?

**9:50 a.m.** A possible chocolaholic was cited at an I Street cooperative supermarket on suspicion of pocketing gooey goodness.

**12:40 p.m.** Suspected badasses – one with a knife strapped to his side and a beanie on his head – were asked to do their mid-day drinking somewhere other than in front of an F Street supermarket.

**4:04 p.m.** More towering illogic, this time at the F Street supermart, where a traveler left his backpack while he shopped, only to find it riffraff-nabbed when he emerged from the store.

• **Wednesday, October 10 3:24 p.m.** A group of drinkers in a tan camper van positioned themselves next to the playground in Redwood Park and took to whooping it up. The partymobile rumbled away before police arrived.

• **Monday, October 15 10:35 p.m.** Six to eight young men playing hacky sack on an apartment quad on upper H isn't going to be a quiet, genteel event.

• **Tuesday, October 16 3:57 p.m.** A shoplifting suspect in custody at an I Street cooperative supermarket identified himself to police as Ramin Fereydouni. His real name turned out to be Nima Jooyandeh.

• **Wednesday, October 17 12:48 a.m.**
So sloshed was this one alleged drunk
Sidewalking on G Street, he sunk
Picked up near the bank
He was plunked in the tank
Till kidneys could purge out the funk.

**2:03 a.m.** When he writes his autobiography, the white male with long black hair and dirty clothes may or may not include that messy business with the drunken scene by the pizza parlor.

• **Friday, October 19 12:55 a.m.** Refused a drink at the Plaza sports bar, a guy took revenge by breaking a window, which he immediately regretted, apologizing

**9:06 a.m.** After a reported threat, a business was to call police if a certain grandma came back.

**10:39 a.m.** His is a life of torment remotely wrought by soulless sirens – telephone harpies who cruelly tantalize with a ringing receiver on entry to his tiny studio apartment with the shared bathroom. But beyond the tinkling piezoelectric ringer lies a mocking vacuum of silence, overturning all rationale for being, hammering heart and soul with a gut-jab of stillborn yearning and a withering blast of broken expectations. The baleful click of a hangup on the other end of the line a mute, grinning death's head beckoning an eternity of sensory deprivation, loneliness and end to hope itself. Other times, alone in the orange-carpeted cubicle, striving to put out of mind the sordid certainty that one's semi-feral kitchenmates are whooping it up under a hail of rap tune artillery, gathered around and guzzling with licentious abandon at the lukewarm forty you just put in the community fridge to chill, like a coven of bloodthirsty hyenas slavering at the sundered bosom of a slain fawn, probably directly from the bottle. A sudden, unseemly lunge at the laughing $19.95 Radio Shack marketing division decision, hoping against reason that its sine-wave warble presages cheery greetings from a familiar voice – friendship, affirmation, redemption. But no. His next move was to call the phone company.

**2:20 p.m.** A fellow doffed his jacket at the Redwood Park basketball court to shoot some hoops, and the garment soon encased a sticky-fingered opportunist.

**11:02 p.m.** A fake I.D. don't even work at the back door of a Plaza tavern.

• **Saturday, October 20 3:55 p.m.** There not being a pit bull, doberman, alligator or wild boar available, a person unleashed his rottweiler in Redwood Park, where traditional families fear to tread.

• **Sunday, October 21 11:26 a.m.** Model Marsh and Wildlife Sanctuary users – camouflage-clad hunters with an unleashed dog – were reported, but couldn't be found.

**5:19 p.m.** A streetside soiree centered around a van at Fifth and

L streets was reported by someone tired of finding discarded needles in the area. An officer found no druggie doings, but warned the party crew for trespassing.

• **Monday, October 22 7:47 p.m.** Every day the Stewart Avenue resident tossed a few more coins in the big jar, and it was adding up. But dreams of a mini-spending spree were dashed when someone stole that big jar of change.

**9:22 p.m.** Conquest-hungry menfolk shared knuckle sandwiches in the 700 block of Seventh Street.

• **Tuesday, October 23 1:56 a.m.** The Ninth Street carport of adventure, romance and petty crime gained a mysterious subplot as an apartment dweller heard someone banging on the walls, possibly with pipes, and indistinct voices. Police found no interlopers, just a tantalizing clue – a set of janitor's keys. But all was secure.

**5:33 p.m.** In a case of irresistible force versus immovable object, someone reportedly tried to run someone else over in a school parking lot. "She did not move out of the way, he did not hit her," states the police report.

**5:49 p.m.** A mom brought her child to APD to have some handcuffs removed.

• **Wednesday, October 24 6:07 p.m.** The owner of the customized, two-story, psychedelically painted and surpassingly groovy school bus with VW van appurtenances may have thought the fanciful contraption would sort of blend right in with the brown fence next to the PG&E substation on Sixth Street during a night's illegal stay there, but no. An officer pointed out relevant sections of the Municipal Code.

**6:35 p.m.** The two travelers had three dogs between them, one of which lifted its leg on the H Street business. That accomplished, the quintet moved along in search of hydrological replenishment.

• **Thursday, October 25 1:03 p.m.** Sure, your family is dysfunctional, and you have stories. But the nuclear household imbroglio of the week was probably the residence wherefrom a woman requested police asistance in leaving, followed by a man's plea for aid with a female in-law who had gone off her meds – way off – and needed help he could not give her. Police confirmed the discontinuance of medications, and after everyone beseeched her to self-commit, she did. It all took only 27 minutes.

**6:22 p.m.** A sidewalk sitter clad in a street vogue – gray camo, a backpack and jaunty hat – plopped down at Ninth and H and, said a witness, set up shop slinging nugs. The pot part wasn't verified, but the open alcohol container – now that was a problem.

• **Friday, October 26 5:13 p.m.** The he-she argument overheard by neighbors escalated into a sentence of outright banishment from the household. "Get out!" she shrieked.

**5:32 p.m.** Another *restraino complaino* in Northtown, where He Who Must Stay Away was allegedly seen driving past her house.

• **Saturday, October 27 9:54 a.m.** A person went walking in the Community Forest near Fickle Hill Road with six dogs, none on leashes. Were anyone to suggest that this was unfair to other forest users, they'd be seriously outnumbered – and outfanged. Animal Control couldn't find the dog pack.

• **Sunday, October 28 1:18 a.m.** An officer peered into the telltale digital readout of a decibel meter at a boisterous Plaza tavern. News from the digital Magic 8-ball was not good.

**7:06 a.m.** After things got hitty between a McKinleyville couple, she was lodged in an Arcata motel. Natch, he started showing up there and was warned away on pain of trespassing. An officer allowed as how he'd probably hang on to those guns for a while, just to be on the safe side. A restraining order was due the next day.

**3:53 p.m.** The soul-pulverizing so-called music blasting down from the apartment above sent him to the phone. An officer found things quiet upstairs, with one individual studying in his room. Roomates had left the residence with the music on, carelessly expending electrons to dubious purpose. All was quiet on departure.

**4:11 p.m.** The letter she received bore a Humboldt County Jail return address, but was postmarked in a Southern California city. Inside was some white powder, and a note which invoked the inspiring term, "Anthrax bitch."

**5:32 p.m.** Some who read of Arcata from afar envy us for having deer show up downtown from time to time, such as in the 1100 block of 11th Street. The Ford lost a headlight; the deer pranced away in an unknown state.

• **Monday, October 29 1:57 p.m.** Egad – could someone in the 1500 block of 11th Street have been... *smoking marijuana?*

**5:37 p.m.** Not only did the scarf 'n' scrammer do a gulp 'n' galumph at a Northtown Chinese restaurant, but he took the leftovers, too. Last seen in a red ball cap toting a white go-box full of congealed pork and rice remnants.

**11:29 p.m.** Some kind of squalid interaction went down between a bar patron and a gollum. The latter creature took his leave by slithering out the door and over the cyclone fence in front of Tavern Row's "missing tooth" empty lot. An eerie play of light and shadow in the trees up at 13th and F streets suggested something half-seen, but turned out to be nothing, nothing at all. Back at the bar, the victim reported a dropped wallet, but nothing was missing.

• **Tuesday, October 30 2:35 a.m.** He couldn't go back to

Seattle, not after skipping that court date. Pallid laundromat lights cast frozen gray light over the dank torpor of his supine being. A uniform... his own voice heard as if from far away... and freezing feet again bore their torpid burden in an uncertain direction.

**9:26 a.m.** Suspected criminal masterminds engineered a daring heist of some brew from an F Street supermarket, which they spirited away to a low-effort remove – the back loading ramp – for undignified glugging. Greasy sleeves dragged across foam-flecked mouths as a blue-and-white APD cruiser rolled up. That one dude went to the Pink House on a warrant while the other two got off after feigning earnest nods.

**10:48 p.m.** In the preternatural paradise off to the side of an F Street pizza parlor's parking lot, goodtimers took their midmorning marijuana break.

• **Halloween 9:11 a.m.** A report of a "loose dog tied to a post" in the 600 block of F Street drew an officer. The owner removed the dual-state doggie.

**8:36 p.m.** An upper H Street residence was reported burgled, though nothing appeared to have been taken. Whoever it was had entered and left a thank you note.

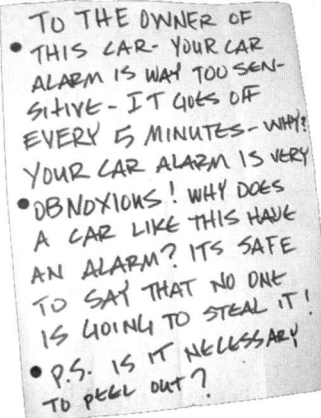

**Cars offer a handy platform for written redress of grievances.**

**11:40 p.m.** Party parking was at a premium on vehicle-choked Eye Street. *Hey,* deduced one circling celebrant, *my car would fit just fine on that neighbor's lawn.*

• **Thursday, November 1 2:41 a.m.** A classic combination – yelling, followed by a thud – was heard on Airstream Avenue. A male person was arrested on three outstanding misdemeanor warrants.

**11:12 a.m.** Anyone who braved the cinderblock and stainless steel elegance of the reeky-creepy public bathroom at the Intermodal Transient Facility would have encountered mind-altering graffiti, swiftly removed at continuing taxpayer expense.

**4:07 p.m.** Three menfolk scarfed $40 worth at a Janes Road chain restaurant and drove away in a silver Dodge Omni without paying their bill. No word on the tip.

• **Friday, November 2 3:05 p.m.**
A father whose daughter cut school
Then challenged her swain to a duel
Police said the threat
Was a foolhardy bet
But restraint orders work as a rule.

• **Saturday, November 3 1:34 a.m.** Someone took a little stroll on top of a car parked on Stromberg Avenue, denting the hood.

**10:26 a.m.** Men came to blows on the Plaza. Someone saw someone start the fight and push another someone. Talk of restraining orders filled the air, along with the usual roaring of engines and nostril-singeing exhaust fumes.

**11:16 a.m.** Hostilities flared again on the Plaza 'twixt the previously encountered irascibles.

**3:27 p.m.** Loose dogs briefly controlled the small park on

Union Street, temporarily extending their hegemony beyond the 14th Street entrance to Redwood Park.

**4:14 p.m.** A gray-haired man perhaps in his late fifties hung out all day at a Northtown eatery, making no purchases and refusing to leave, creeping out the minimally compensated staff. Yet when police came, he was gone.

**9:26 p.m.** An Anina Way downstairs resident complained of the thunderous nature of the televised sporting experience going on upstairs. Police thought the volume acceptable, but forwarded the complaint.

**10:07 p.m.** Now it was downstairs' turn to share high-volume hockey video adventure with upstairsians. A fan agreed to attenuate the puckage.

**• Tuesday, November 13 2:13 p.m.** A youth reportedly locked himself in the bathroom, and, according to APD, his mother stated she'd "beat the shit" out of the kid. Police and family members did what they could to forestall mom-induced release of the lad's contents.

**• Wednesday, November 14 9:16 p.m.** Tender expressions of love, over time, evolved into more somewhat more staccato declarations of I'm-gonna-throw-all-your-shit-away, jerk. Officers stood by with their hands on their belts while he humped his stuff out to the waiting Firebird.

**9:38 p.m.** A fellow out carousing along Tavern Row mistook a car for a urinal, which made the owner a tad curious. He asked the urinator about the matter, but the peesome geek became irate and allegedly socked the car owner in the jaw, then scampered across the Plaza. Police tracked the dashing figure, resplendent in baseball cap and sweatshirt tied around his waist, to a since-closed nightclub and admonished him. The owner of the urine-soaked conveyance said just forget it.

• **Thursday, November 15 10:21-10:35 a.m.** People who go around in the middle of the night looking in cars for valuables and taking whatever they find always have ready work. On Bayside Road, a color TV left overnight in a back seat disappeared through a jimmied door.

**4:46 p.m.** Pete sat for a time in an apartment doorway on Samoa Boulevard, then did his shambling thing.

**7:27 p.m.** A knave deemed unfit to populate a taqueria was expelled from same.

• **Friday, November 16 12:58 p.m.** A McKinleyville youth reportedly jumped up and down on a ping pong table on west End Road, rendering it unusable.

**3:08 p.m.** Woebetide anyone who unknowingly wanders into the public dope bazaar known as the 14th Street Redwood Park parking lot to enjoy the natural values without benefit of cannabis impairment. There, surly clutches of bedraggled folk press little smokestacks to their faces, blow bong hits in their dogs' faces and, if eye contact isn't avoided, ask for money. Ain't nature grand?

• **Saturday, November 17 10:14 p.m.** A woman called to say her mother, born in 1916, left a bus in Eureka and got into a pickup truck with persons unknown.

**11:11 p.m.** A Heather Lane resident believed a piece of salmon had been left out by a neighbor in a deliberate attempt to kill her dog dead.

• **Sunday, November 18 12:27 a.m.** A person's ability to rove around town in a couple thousand pounds of hurtling steel was curtailed when police suspected certain blood chemistry anomalies consistent with cocktail glugging in the 700 block of 14th Street.

**1:28 a.m.** Still another, but this time the alleged drunken driver in the 700 block of Samoa Boulevard barricaded himself in the vehicle, evidently on the woozy presumption that police would just give up and go away.

**2:30 a.m.** A woman had a little question for some people being loud next door to her home in the 1600 block of 11th Street. "Do you know what time it is?" she asked. Thence came the witty ripost, in the form of a question: "Do you know what kind of gun I have?" Though the outcome isn't documented, the potential for serious jeopardy was apparently not fully realized.

**4:03 p.m.** The allure of fragrant baked goods allegedly overcame one young man's ethical constraints at an I Street cooperative supermarket. He was citizen's arrested.

**11:19 p.m.** A tangled web of intrigue in Valley West included a guy at a pay phone informing what a witness surmised was a girl at the other end of the line that he was, in so many words, going to kill her. "I'll kill you!" he said, slamming the phone down, striking it and sustaining possible hand injuries, then stalking off toward the credit union. Meanwhile, a car was observed "parked kind of odd" behind a liquor store with a woman in the passenger seat. Coincidence, maybe. Lynchian, certainly.

**• Monday, November 19 8:41 – 10:03 a.m.** A devil wind came up, blowing down power lines in the 100 block of 13th Street and the 800 block of 11th Street, working juju on motion sensors at homes and businesses and triggering false alarms like the one in the 200 block of Bayside Road.

**2:25 p.m.** These guys used to be really tight, but bad energy now rules their encounters.

**3:43 p.m.** A man in a red parka fell out of the window in an unrented Valley West motel room and ran away.

**7:41 p.m.** Dogs barked like crazy on Iverson Avenue right until a cop car rolled up.

**10:12 p.m.** This time their police radar failed them and the Iverson dogs' owner and his dad spoke with police. The owner was told he would be getting rid of his arfsome charges.

• **Tuesday, November 20 2:28 a.m.** A recidivist *homo sapien* took it upon himself to smash the window in the lovely kiosk at a G Street art deco movie theater.

**10:55 a.m.** A goat went for a little goat stroll on Susan Avenue.

**1:12 p.m.** Someone thought different about an Apple laptop computer in the 600 block of Sixth Street, as in it wasn't theirs but they took it home anyway. A big loss to the business from which it was stolen, too, as its hard drive contained lots of crucial information.

**5:45 p.m.**
A Cedar Drive motorist passed
A chap who, with consummate class
Displayed his behind
The moon*ee*, more refined
Could have done without seeing his ass.

**5:54 p.m.** Another charmer – a big fat guy guzzling a forty from a bag – set up a customer harassment station in front of a business in the 900 block of I Street. He strode away but was contacted by an officer, who found him beery but not blotto.

**6:02 p.m.** Two exes traded accusations of telephone harassment, but the interpersonal imbroglio that took years to create defied immediate police solution.

**8:59 p.m.** A distraught, weeping woman appeared at APD, but before anyone could talk to her she was gone, next appearing at a supermarket across the street. There, it looked to an officer like she might be *on something*, and her narrative did little to dispell that impression. She claimed that a uniformed Navy officer absconded with her purse over at the bus station. He than gave it to another man, she said, who handed off the handbag to yet another unknown – possibly imaginary – man at the supermarket. Employees there didn't see anyone with her purse, and at that point, the officer pretty much abandoned hope of sorting it all out.

• **Wednesday, November 21 5:55 p.m.** A fellow who'd recently and repeatedly put cup to lip placed himself next to an F Street pet shop and took to yelling and hitting himself. He was trundled off to the tank until the beverages wore off.

**9:14 p.m.** Child custody exchanges are often transacted in very public places on the theory that pent-up resentments will remain suppressed with strangers around for the few moments it takes to hand off the kid(s). But that doesn't stop antagonists from getting off piercing rejoinders such as the one a former father-in-law was alleged to have aimed at a despised former son-in-law during a child-swap at a downtown coffee temple. "I'm warning you to lay off my daughter," the angered dad reportedly said. "You haven't seen my dark side yet. You're going to get *seriously fucked*." An officer deemed this utterance something short of a terrorist threat, and offered to stand by the next day when the child was returned.

• **Thursday, November 22 6:59 p.m.** Once one of Arcata's most popular nomadic campgrounds, the public toilet at the Intermodal Transient Facility is now behind steel bars at night. Unknown forces penetrated the outer barrier, but the inside door held.

• **Friday, November 23 9:20 p.m.** Mobile morons in a white car threatened a passerby in an I Street alley.

• **Saturday, November 24 2:57 a.m.** The lower reaches of desolate South G Street form a jagged post-industrial landscape gradually returning to its original wetland state. Rusting hulks of machinery flake away atop cracked, dissipating pavement which occasionally flickers with the streaking shadows of migratory waterfowl making their way up and down the Pacific Flyway. And in that land of contrasts, two men came to blows, duking it out in the middle of the darkened roadway. But in keeping with the South G theme of ugliness ceding to beauty, the men abandoned aggression in favor of affection, and were next observed hugging – like *real* men.

**5:12 p.m.** Another man set up a female harassment station in front of a business in the 900 block of G Street. Officers caught up with him down the way, and warned him about that kind of thing, as in don't come back, ever.

• **Sunday, November 25 11:52 a.m.** The staccato narrative of the APD dispatcher log seems to indicate that someone stole the trunk lid off an old Camaro parked out in Valley West.

• **Monday, November 26 12:53 p.m.** Personnel at a Ninth Street hardware store asked the person sleeping in their cardboard recycling bin over and over again to get outta there, but he wouldn't. A higher, bluer form of persuasion was called in.

**2:24 p.m.** A traveler overstayed his welcome at an I Street bagelry, and was slow to get the message to make like a tree.

**2:27 p.m.** Bill and Virgil must have done up some really dank-o-matic bud. After all, how stoned and lethargic do you have to be to get busted for possesh in the 14th Street Redwood Park lot?

**2:32 p.m.** A panic alarm went off at a health care facility in the 1600 block of Weott Way. Police called the place, and the person on the line said, "Oh, did we hit the button again?" with laughter overheard in the background. *Tee-hee, aren't we cute to waste the time and resources of emergency personnel?* An officer checked the place, making sure everything was OK.

**2:41 p.m.** Kids getting off a school bus on Union Street witnessed a man on an apartment balcony across the street who was yelling and pouring beer over his head. Unspecified "stuff" was hanging off the balcony, and the guy went in and out of his shared kitchen, yelling. Visiting his apartment, the self-basting beer brandisher appeared to have mental problems but wasn't committable.

**4:43 p.m.** The Aggressive Panhandler of the Year Award

goes to the man at the Post Office who demanded money from patrons, even following them to their cars and blocking entry until they paid his toll. Police advised him to move along.

**7:07 p.m.** Unhappy with her hairstyling experience, a visitor from San Francisco up and walked out of a Plaza salon. The stylist pursued her, and police caught up with the two at Seventh and F streets. The customer then offered to pay $45 of the $60 beautification fee, then to return to the shop and allow the stylist to repair the beauty damage, at which time she'd pay the balance. The stylist was concerned that the customer was trying to weasel out of the whole fee, but after some mediation by an officer, an agreement was reached.

• **Wednesday, November 28 8:56 a.m.** An officer interviewed a person mingling at the open-air dope bazaar known as the 14th Street Redwood Park parking lot.

**12:30 p.m.** A traveler said he'd been assaulted and injured by someone named "Motrin" on the Plaza the previous day. Though he'd run away when police had arrived in response to the fight call, he now wanted justice levied against the pain-relieving pain-inflicter. He asked an officer to take Polaroids of his injuries and give him the pictures. An officer agreed to take pictures, but said he'd keep them as evidence. This didn't work for the victim, who left.

• **Thursday, November 29 6:48 p.m.** Just what a downtown office building needed (or maybe not): a front door greeter with long, shaggy brown hair and a missing front tooth, talking to himself, harassing passersby and refusing to leave. Police reality-checked him, but didn't have a lot to work with.

• **Friday, November 30 8:11 a.m.** A traveler who employees at an F Street supermarket said had ripped off some cigarettes followed up by being uncooperative and abusive to the help. Cigarettes aren't allowed in the Pink House, so as one can readily see, his was a fool's errand and he was the man for the job.

**2:34 p.m.** It looked really suspicious the way them skinny dudes was rummaging through the bags of stuff in the alley behind Tavern Row. Approached, they barked out something rude and slunk away all sketchy-like. Maybe the stuff is stolen... and isn't that guy a doper? As it happened, the property was his – he was just storing it there in the urinary alley and drugs weren't an issue.

**10:46 p.m.** Another in the seemingly limitless available pool of semi-feral wanderers with nothing else to do reportedly entered a Northtown motel, erupted with racial comments and threats of violence, then headed out to that byway of lost souls, the pedestrian overpass. Police offered a stern warning which included the terms "if you return," "trespass" and "arrest," some of which may have penetrated the spurious electrical traffic ricocheting about his cranium.

**10:44 p.m.** An Alliance Road resident saw a dirty-looking 20-something guy take a whiz by her house, but when he realized he was being seen, he took off, only to return a half-hour later. He wanted not just to talk, but with his public excretory demonstration an example of his manners, to be allowed in her apartment as well. She said no, closed then locked the door. It sounded like he was trying the knob with his unwashed hands, but when police arrived he had wandered away.

**• Saturday, December 1 3:36 a.m.** It's a thin line between love and things being slammed against a wall, pounding on a door and rocks being thrown at a window in the 100 block of Bayside Road.

**12:50 p.m.** The guy in the wheelchair is always toking in highly public places. So maybe he has a 215 license, cool, but it's still jarring to see someone ingesting a mood drug in the street. Would a little discretion peril the Bill of Rights?

**3:53 p.m.** A traveler chugged a brew in the 800 block of G Street.

**9:46 p.m.** Travelers chugged pot in the 800 block of Ninth Street.

**11:01 p.m.** Someone called 911, uttered a traveler's name and hung up. Police went to 14th and G street and arrested the person named on suspicion of offering false information, placing him on a parole hold.

**• Sunday, December 2 12:01 p.m.** When you're King of the Road, at the wheel of an all-powerful Black Ford Excursion, you find your mighty steed thirstier than the old wallet can handle, and it's time for an ignominious fill 'n' flee at a Valley West gas station.

**10:04 p.m.** A "scraggly" 20-something in dark flannel went into a minor H Street movie theatre, reached over the counter and grabbed a bag of money, then fled with all his might down Isaac Minor Alley and past the bagel shop.

**• Monday, December 3 1:29 a.m.** There was some cocaine – who knows how much? – lost somewhere in the house, and we all know what a gosh-darn nuisance that can be. A woman tried to calm them down, and she and one of the cokehunters were to go for a change of scenery.

**7:02 p.m.**
Dreads and plastic jacket
By the railroad tracks
Deep in conversation
No one there to answer back.

There they found a fellow
Clad in a vinyl mac
But otherwise non-wonky
Left to his solo act.

**10:16 a.m.** Civilization has degenerated to the point where you'd best take your exterior glass in every night unless you want it etched like the east-facing window in the 1100 block of 11th Street.

**1:26 p.m.** It was theorized that there may have been a health and safety violation (read: drugs) behind what seemed a bit of an overreaction to what began with a Christmas tree star allegedly being hung upside down and led to a threat, then a solo sprint across a grassy field. Outcome undocumented.

• **Tuesday, November 4 Noon** Interpersonal hostility blossomed like a demon orchid nourished by hell's acrid vapours bursting obscenely through the pavement in the south lot of an historic Plaza building, bearing foul petals of burning rubber and jutting pistils like venom-loaded syringes. But his consternation stemmed not from tortured metaphors. No it was an illegal u-turn committed right before his eyes which compelled him to personally take the violator to task, vigilante-style. An officer advised the justice-seeker that it's not a good idea to confront strangers in the street. Everyone went away and peace befell the land once more, until the next statistically inevitable bozo eruption.

• **Wednesday, December 5 8:26 p.m.** His reality included enjoying a cigar after a satisfying dinner at a Plaza hotel, whereupon an unknown woman whom he never touched exited the hotel and grabbed both his cigar and his glasses. Her reality involved an unfamiliar man standing in front of the hotel who "grabbed her." She refused any further detail, but insisted her future be grope-free from cigar-wielding strangers.

• **Friday, December 7** Someone reported a "bear's head" – obviously a euphemism for something else – on the east side of G Street under the pedestrian walkway. There, an Arcata park ranger discovered... the actual head of an *ursus americanus*. "It was fresh," said Ranger Bob. "Within 48 hours. I thought at first it might have rolled off somebody's truck." No other bear parts were found in the area, and the bear's manner of death – poached or permitted – is not known. The head was turned over to the state Department of Fish and Game for documentation and disposal.

• **Saturday, December 8 8:37 a.m.** A neighborhood market was purchased by an East Indian family, and two days later it was tagged with graffiti that suggested a potential hate incident.

**10 a.m.** Someone entered a Lewis Avenue resident's backyard and cut down a small pine tree, but couldn't get it over the fence.

**10:49 a.m.** A man alleged that his ex suckerpunched him in a Plaza tavern in the wee hours of this day, and she said yep, she sure did.

**12:54 p.m.** Several ad hoc arboreal activists were discovered planting trees in the party meadow/dog run at Redwood Park. They said they had the City Manager's permish, but he said no way, and that they ought to just leave. Ultimately, it was determined that the silly boys were climbing the trees, not planting them, though it's difficult to understand how anyone could confuse those two activities.

**1:59 p.m.** The semi-feral leisure specialists who hang around the free food trough across from the Intermodal Transient Facility – the indolent male variety, that is – decided to harass hapless womenfolk in the area. Someone called the cops, the manly men scattered like the roaches they so assiduously strive to emulate. Just the facts.

• **Sunday, December 9 4:35 a.m.** Asking why the guy on Hallen Drive called 911 and hung up at 4:35 a.m. is probably pointless – he doesn't even know. An APD dispatcher called the number back, but there was no answer. Moments later, however, a *69 call came in from the place; the caller evidently trying to ascertain who'd just rang the phone he dared not pick up. To his chagrin, it was APD! He was evasive, and blamed it on "one of the kids running around the house." Uh-*huh*, said police. *Kids*, eh? It's 4:35 a.m. "I'm from down south," he said, his vestigial cred melting away beneath his feet. "Just visiting." Put one of the "kids" on the line. You know, the ones running around dialing 911? Silence. So what's really going on there, bub? "Everything's fine." *Click.*

**11:49 a.m.** Another pointless interpersonal fuss involving the household with the lost cocaine. This time, a dead-end dust-up was over who could park where outside.

• **Monday, December 10 7:59 a.m.** If only you could leave a cell phone in an unlocked car in Patrick Court and have it be there the next morning, what a wonderful wonderful world this would be.

**2:54 p.m.** A girl wrote a poem which compelled police to have a word with her parents.

• **Tuesday, December 11 3:12 a.m.** APD helped HSUPD with someone who turned up on the floor of the lobby of the university police station clad in plastic bags.

**12:11–12:22 a.m.** A park ranger held productive discussions with inhabitants of the 14th Street Redwood Park lot and surrounding environs. He then took a little stroll in the heavily impacted lower forest to meet and greet the hobbits, trolls and other less-benevolent life forms present.

• **Friday, December 14 1:23 a.m.** It's such a placid tavern, with all the kitschy furnishings and dead animal heads staring dully at patrons kibbitzing in jovial fashion as C&W twangs from the jukebox. So when a customer threw a glass at the bar and tried to pick fights with the other patrons, well, naturally he stood out a bit. He was arrested and jailed on a probation violation beef.

**6:02 p.m.** Protesters objecting to an unspecified issue – *what, like there's anything wrong with the world these days?* – were asked to stay out of traffic at Ninth and H streets.

• **Saturday, December 15 12:46 a.m.** Another urine donor – this one wearing a sweatshirt bearing the legend "Independence" – drenched the side of a downtown brewery and scampered away toward the Plaza.

**3:11 a.m.** Someone unknown was heard trying a doorknob on Shirley Avenue. It was locked, so they left. But if it *hadn't* been?

**5:11 p.m.** An SUV was packed heavily "for a trip to Hawaii," said a caller, and had been stolen. The victim named a theft suspect, whom he said may have been headed north to McKinleyville to drive the vehicle into the ocean, perhaps attempting to reach the intended destination by surface route. Outcome undocumented.

• **Monday, December 17 8:12 a.m.** A guy in a white sweatshirt was reported outside the high school, directing students to where they could obtain that excellent fact-retention enabler known as marijuana. The stone-ager eluded detection.

**5:36 p.m.** A hunter communed with nature by blowing the heads off passing wildlife after restricted hours not far from the Marsh and Wildlife Sanctuary.

• **Tuesday, December 18 12:50 a.m.** An argument between agitated menfolk on lower F Street included the statement *"I'm not going back to jail!"* Police rolled up; there was some fence-jumping and hiding in bushes, and everyone was released to carry on with not going back to jail.

**12:59 p.m.** Someone accused a Northtown erotic supply depot of selling nitrous oxide to minors, the inhalation of which gas is a refined pastime suitable only for discerning adults wishing for a one-minute braingasm. As walls lined with shrink-wrapped, glowering hussies and bins brimming with crudely wrought plastic dicks shimmered in the fluorescent light waiting patiently for the untoward attentions of willing suitors, an employee was advised of the complaint.

**2:26 p.m.** Off-leash dogs are a potentially serious problem, as anyone keeping up with current events well knows. But chasing someone around Stewart Park and shrieking at them and Fido may not be the optimal method for addressing the matter.

**9:31 p.m.** A dog had an arf-tastic evening on Blakeslee Avenue.

• **Wednesday, December 19 5:41 a.m.** A man stood outside an Old Arcata Road market, apparently practicing putting on and taking off his raincoat and by doing so, unnerving others. Advised of the complaint, he moved along.

• **Monday, December 24 2:52 p.m.** A brown '85 Chevy

pickup with a camper shell was left unlocked in the 1100 block of 12th Street with the keys inside, and someone decided to take it for the low, low everyday price of free.

**4:04 p.m.** A car full of young jackals ran a stop sign, almost running someone over, then pulling into a mortuary parking lot and braying with hilarity over nearly sending the pedestrian to that or a similar facility. The victim got the plate, and a letter was sent to the registered jackass.

**4:39 p.m.** A Laurel Drive resident reported hearing a woman scream and someone get stabbed upstairs. Also, reported the caller, none of the cars in the apartment building's parking lot have required permits. Four times in the last two days, he said, he saw "hands passing drugs in baggies." Queried, he couldn't really explain why he thought the woman had been stabbed. An officer checked the area and found nothing suspicious.

• **Christmas Day 2:20 a.m.** Instead of spending his wee hours snuggled up in bed eagerly anticipating the arrival of Santa, something named Nathan was reported trying to get in the back door of a Ninth Street address. He was arrested on a public drunkenness charge.

**2:54 a.m.** Maybe the party animals on Trojan Street were trying to establish a sonic homing beacon for reindeer, but all it attracted was cops.

• **Wednesday, December 26 6:06 a.m.** An alleged drunk was scraped out of Redwood Park near the Redwood Lodge and taken to a ghastly Pink building in Eureka which felt as though it was mounted on a spinning platform.

• **Saturday, December 29 4:23 a.m.** The Bickersons of South G Street did their part to pathos-ize this week's log. She called police saying he was holding a knife and threatening suicide. He was heard in the background telling her to "cut it out"

and yelling that he was fine. Police traveled the well-worn route
to the residence. There was no indication that anything like what
she had described had actually occurred, so she was sent home.

## • Sunday, December 30 3:10 p.m.
A little encampment of four
Hung out by the hardware store door
Their drums started throbbin'
While they was hobnobbin'
Till asked to not be there no more.

**10:20 p.m.** This interview in the alley behind a Plaza tavern
was more or less typical of the numbskullian wastes of time
distracting public safety personnel on the cusp of the new
year. Numerous other encounters and interviews centering
on alcohol-related wacky misadventures were to follow
throughout the downtown area.

## • New Year's Day 2002 11:25 a.m.
An underwear drawer
may not offer the Fort Knox-like security one assumes, and
certainly nothing approaching the sock drawer's vault-like
impregnability. A Buttermilk Lane resident is out $300.

**12:18 a.m.** A woman's head collided with a bottle on the Plaza's
west side, requiring an ambulance trip. No word on the bottle.

**1:31 p.m.** Underwear inspires not just thieves, but those whose
love life revolves around telephones and strangers. Four times a
woman was called by an unknown person who asked, "What kind
of underpants are you wearing?" She decided to get Caller I.D.

**5:32 p.m.** 2002 got off to an auspicious start on Canyon Road, where
neighbor turned upon neighbor over three to four oranges which had
been thrown at someone's house. Suspected citrus slingers denied it,
and another neighbor wasn't aware of any fruit-based aggression.

**9:30 p.m.** A freeloader with a mole on the left side of his face schlupped up $13.53 in adult beverages at a Plaza tavern. He and his beauty mark then wove their way out the door without paying.

**11:44 p.m.** Several folks and twice as many fists were reported in a squabble near Apartment 27. A woman retrieved children's clothes from the home and left.

• **Thursday, January 3 3:13 a.m.** A patient who had been medically cleared refused to leave the hospital, saying he couldn't walk. "I can't walk," he said. And yet, whether due to divine intervention, positive thinking or the excitement of the inevitable next encounter with an officer, the fellow somehow sprang to his feet and sauntered away.

**2:01 p.m.** Drunken male gladiators clashed in the 1000 block of Hallen Drive, with a parking lot serving as their Coliseum. They then fled in a yellow van-chariot.

• **Friday, January 4 2:42 a.m.** Back to the South G conflict corral, where quarrels and unverifiable claims continue 'round the clock. A woman said that a fellow at the center of numerous previous calls to police had removed pieces of her piano. Police arrived and tried to contact the woman, but she refused to answer the door and only mumbled unintelligibly through it, which hardly helped police elucidate the truth of the caper.

**3:14 a.m.** You were home in bed, missing a grand opportunity for recreation along Tavern Row. But not this fellow in baggy pants and a white jacket, who created a fuss sufficient for police to arrest him on a public intoxication charge.

**7:32 a.m.**
A former motel employee
In Valley West, Room 243
Shouldn't have, but used a key
To spend the night inside for free.
Then headed north, back to B.C.

• **Saturday, January 5 12:06 p.m.** Me and you and a drug named Boo, travelin' and a-doin' bong hits in the Redwood Park meadow and a-gettin' cited by Arcata's own Danger Ranger.

When the amazing pipe known as "Nebula" was confiscated by Ranger Bob in Redwood Park, a short-lived "Free Nebula" movement coalesced, only to disperse in the cosmic winds of interstellar space.

**12:39 p.m.** Meanwhile just down the way, another traveler had the very original notion that her unlicensed dog ought to romp and poop freely through picnics and playgrounds in Redwood Park. A citation reality-checked her and her canine charge.

**4:11 p.m.** A guy went nuclear in front of an F Street supermarket because of a life-changing setback involving the pay phone keeping his quarter. He was advised to go away.

**6:23 p.m.** A resident in one of the shared-kitchen-and-bathroom studio apartments at a Union Street residential inn was reported trying to force the door to a neighboring flat. He and a fellow resident explained that "they wanted to see what it looked like inside." Well, let's just save you the Breaking and Entering charge – it looks exactly like *your* dismal cubicle, m'boy.

• **Sunday, January 6 12:17 a.m.** Another uplifting

encounter in one of the pink fourplexes on Heather Lane, where those in Apartment 3 were reported pounding on the walls, and not in a quiet way, either. A neighbor went to their door and was rewarded with a neighborly fusillade of profanity, as did another nearby resident. An officer met with the person in 3, where things were quiet for the moment. But when the cop began to leave, the noise started up again. The guy then said he wanted to accuse someone of breaking his door, but there was no evidence of that.

**3:39 a.m.** Where love once blossomed like a febrile flower in a halo of dewdrops like tender kisses, now she said he'd busted her windshield and "thrashed" her apartment. Then she admitted she'd broken his windshield, and declined to make any report.

**4:48 a.m.** Near Foster Avenue one man was heard to tell another, "Be a man and have a good night." A minute later a woman was heard screaming. Police checked the area; nothing.

**1:16 p.m.** A man's leashed dog, being walked on Beverly Drive, was reportedly attacked by two loose dogs. A witness said he called the owner of the loose dogs a "bitch" and threw a stick on her lawn to even the score. His dog supposedly required veterinary treatment. Police interviewed all involved.

**3:22 p.m.** On Olympia Street, folks were said to be turning their music up real loud, then down, then up, then down over and over. Police recommended that they focus on the "down" part.

**3:59 p.m.** A woman was reported having "problems or difficulties" with her son, with few specifics other than that he was making a mess and she wanted him arrested. That didn't happen, but the incident was documented.

**8:42 p.m.** A brother and sister from out of town got into an huge argument at a Valley West motel where they were staying – well, actually there were staying behind it, in their car – over whether to allow a cat out of the vehicle. They were warned about camping and left the area with tabby in tow.

• **Tuesday, January 8 4:42 p.m.** It's the fab new fad – take Postal Service address stickers, scribble your tag on it and then stick it on public appurtenances. This was seen happening in Northtown, and a youth was identified. Mom and Dad got the call.

**5:34 p.m.** In retrospect, it would've been better for the bicyclist to have actually, you know, *stopped* at the Eighth and G streets stop sign.

**9:43 p.m.** A major *ka-boom!* and a cloud of smoke was reported at Poplar Drive and Ponderosa Way. Yet an officer found nothing there.

**10:13 p.m.** A Fortuna woman drove all the way to Arcata to be arrested on a DUI charge.

• **Wednesday, January 9 12:13 a.m.** A dad 'n' lad shout-out, then beddie-bye for both.

**12:31 a.m.** Cows briefly escaped human oppression near Anvick Road, then relented and will soon be coming to a hamburger near you.

**8:28 a.m.** Clods stapled handbills into the plaster wall of a 10th Street brewery, A Janes Road sports bar adjunct to a chain restaurant was contacted. It related the complaint to the bands and their staple gun-armed minions.

**5:16 p.m.** Tensions at a Union Street residential inn exploded, with hearty helpings of knuckle sandwich served up in the shared kitchen which serves as an odor-retention airlock between cubicles. Police verified a verbal disagreement 'twixt innmates, but neither wished to pursue the matter.

**7:43 p.m.** A vehicle became hung up on the southeast corner of the roundabout – a seeming contradiction in terms, but perhaps the hangup occurred on one of the ancillary channels – at Samoa Boulevard and Buttermilk Lane. At the driver's request, a tow truck was called.

• **Thursday, January 10 10:58 a.m.** Got those old hangin'-out by-the-Radio-Shack-dumpster, drinking-but-not-drunk-enough-for-a-Pink-House-lunch blues.

**8:54 p.m.** Two stylin' dudes sporting hats and goatees left a Valley West night spot and sauntered unsteadily to the nearby motel where they were staying. On the way, they stopped at the Golden Arches for an alcohol-diluting, artery-encumbering snack.

• **Friday, January 11 12:28 a.m.** Three travelers found hanging around the Intermodal Transient Facility were warned about camping, and one cited.

**5:26 p.m.** An officer was flagged down and told of a disoriented woman near Klopp Lake. Another citizen said a woman had been wading into the lake's north side and standing in the water. The officer walked the shoreline and found no indication of anyone wading – the water, for example, was perfectly clear with no particulate turbidity indicative of the lake bed having been disturbed.

**5:42 p.m.** A report of a distraught person at Samoa and I streets led the officer back to Klopp Lake on a report of a woman having walked into the lake. Again the area was checked, but no one found in or around the lake.

**6:14 p.m.** A husband and wife converged on an Alliance Road mini-mart to have a loud public argument, then leave in separate vehicles.

**10:20 p.m.** The proverbial drunk-on-a-long-Greyhound-ride nightmare scenario was not to take place this evening, as the driver just wouldn't let the guy on.

**10:23 p.m.** A group of eight to 10 Sunny Brae youths positioned themselves in the traffic channelization curbs at Crescent Way and Chester Avenue and took to yelling at passing cars. The outcome is undocumented, but they must have dispersed, since they're not there any more.

• **Saturday, January 12 1:51 a.m.** A backwards green hat, multicolored pants and an admonishment to never show his multicolors in an F Street 24-hour supermarket again.

**2:50 a.m.** A man passed out from sheer enjoyment plus a surfeit of cocktail refreshment along Tavern Row. He was scraped from the pavement and redeposited in the county tank till all the happiness was filtered from his bloodstream.

**12:25 p.m.**
Two travelers broke out a nug
And proceeded upon it to chug
But Redwood Park's lot
Is best used without pot
Marijuana's for sick folks – a drug.

**12:44 p.m.** Eight folks on some kind of party-picnic on the railroad tracks near the storage unit yard were warned of a noise complaint, and dispersed.

**1:16 p.m.**
Two more travs in Redwood Park's lot
Unleashed their four-legged pal, Spot
The loosened pooch scampered
Till masters were hampered
By tickets which Ranger Bob wrought.

**1:54-2 p.m.** The selfsame park ranger roamed lower trails, chatting with elves and trolls encountered along the way.

**2:41 p.m.** A neighbor dispute in Valley West centered around the two large flagpoles installed in a front yard. The flags and ropes clang against the poles 24 hours a day.

• **Sunday, January 13 1:51 a.m.** It started in an unspecified Plaza tavern, when one guy thought another had pushed his girlfriend. Instant justice was meted out in the form of a blow to the back of the perceived pusher's head. Corpuscles hit the pavement by the doughnut bar, but he denied police and medical assistance and was taken from the area by two less cocktailed compatriots.

**3:55 a.m.** A man doing his best to impersonate a cop magnet was arrested on suspicion of driving without a license, false registration and an outstanding misdemeanor warrant. The steel bars of the Pink House served to temporarily neutralize the cop-attractant effect.

**1:02 p.m.** More ripoffery at an I Street cooperative supermarket ended in a citation for a suspect.

• **Monday, January 14 11:46 p.m.** Lots of people roughhousing and banging things on Valley East Boulevard – hey, there's not a lot to do in "Gateway to McKinleyville" – agreed to quieten down.

• **Tuesday, January 15 12:08 p.m.** A noon-hour soiree on the train tracks by the storage park was sullied by intra-hobo contretemps. Several crabby goodtimers skulked from the scene bearing another layer of grudgehood.

**2:08 p.m.**
A Redwood Park lot lounger's thirst
Was slaked till things turned for the worst
A ranger soon loomed
Happy hour was doomed
With a ticket, the booze-bubble burst.

**3:15 p.m.** The term "scruffy" is always pregnant with association, usually having to do with grouchy, overbearing spare-changers. You'd think Chapter 1, page 1 of *Panhandling for Dummies* would say something about "Don't growl at people," but this guy, last seen headed towards a downtown coffee temple, apparently hadn't read it.

**3:48 a.m.** Just think – someone born in 1984 is old enough to allegedly shoplift at an I Street cooperative supermarket.

**5:31 p.m.** A large congregation was dispersed from the 14th Street side of Redwood Park. Maybe it was a mass game of charades, a fondue party or an EST seminar. Nah, probably not.

**6:32 p.m.** Mom radar, which rivals NORAD for sensitivity and reach, is usually pretty good at picking up a tot's cries, even over the white noise hiss of a shower. But showerly bliss may have overridden maternal alert mode, and worried neighbors called police. The mixup was quickly resolved.

**6:57 p.m.** Leave, said the barkeep. No, said the drinker. Leave, said the cop. I was just leaving, said the drinker.

• **Wednesday, January 16 3:45 p.m.** A Eureka woman must have had better days. First she has to drive to Arcata to pay a parking ticket, then she twists her ankle in the City Hall parking lot.

**5:46 p.m.** He said $40 had just been stolen from him on the Plaza. Police found no evidence that a theft had occurred, and APD doesn't have a Cash Replacement Program.

**6:47 p.m.**
Four men on L Street
Stopped, whipped it out and unsheathed
Streaming shafts of gold.

# IMBROGLIO EXTRA

# JENNIFER SAVAGE'S STREET MUSICIANS

**Percussionists percolate on the Plaza.**

resident McKinley glows ever stoic in the sunshine. The smell of olive oil, onions and fresh basil emanates from the creperie van. Shoppers wander in and out of record stores, clothing boutiques, lunch spots and an art gallery. The sound of a didjeridoo radiates from within a doorway. Or is it three didjeridoos? A waif and two shabbily dressed men have tucked themselves into a Plaza nook and drone forth.

**"We like a town that's full of music," said Roslyn Imrie as she serenaded Seventh Street.**

Sometimes the music played freely across downtown originates from bagpipes, an instrument that has struck fear in harsher climes and harder hearts than those typically found in A-town.

Most notorious is the incessant rhythm of bongos. Or congas. While the players attain a sort of drum-circle transcendence, those who live and work in listening range become quickly aware of their limits – and just as rapidly reach for the phone. Busting percussionists is all in a day's work for Arcata's police force.

People don't complain as much about the violinist. Perhaps because he usually plays at night, when the responsible and upstanding sorts have tucked away in their homes for the evening. Maybe it's because the sweet and sorrowful tones feel like an appropriate soundtrack for the human drama acted out nightly across the Plaza.

Probably no one grumbles much about the rare flute or stray harmonica. The odd accordion inspires mixed perspectives.

Sometimes the instrument of choice is the common guitar. Street musician Sean Powers sits down on the sidewalk every couple of months, sets out his case to welcome dollars and change, then strums happily for a few hours or until asked to move along. He's migrated from the streets of San Francisco to the corners of Arcata. He thought he'd make more money here. He doesn't, but the people are nicer. "I had some free time," he said of how he got started. "I thought I'd see what happened."

A favorite spot is a street over from the Plaza, in front of Arcata's beloved Los Bagels, a Jewish-Mexican bakery immortalized in the children's book *Jalapeño Bagels* by Natasha Wing. "On a good morning, I make about $15," Powers said. But the income derived by volunteering music varies. "It's totally random," he said. "If it's a nice day, there's a lot of traffic. If it's a nice night, there's usually a lot of people out." He hasn't been hassled by the fuzz too much. "The other day, I saw the police drive by. Then a cop pulled up, and I thought I was in for it – but he just smiled and kept going."

The lines defining the borders between "regular" musicians, "street" musicians and stoned-students-who-happen-to-own-bongos shift as often as the town's Plaza population. During Arts! Arcata, the monthly art-walk event, some of Arcata's finest musicians can be found jamming in front of the upscale furniture store at Eighth and G streets while just down the way, huddled near Jacoby's Storehouse, three unknowns let loose with perhaps not as tight, but still heartfelt tunes good enough that the dollar bills have accumulated in the cardboard box to the side. Everyone's getting paid to make music, so a certain professionalism becomes established, especially during actual events. Random afternoons and nights, the outdoor music scene belongs to those who feel moved to perform, money or no. To some of those who share the area in which those sounds travel, the ("so-called") musicians are a nuisance. To others, they're a blessing. "I love the free music," one Plazagoer shrugged.          – *J.S.*

**Sean Powers, sometime guitarist, with his 100-year-old button concertina.**

• **Friday, January 18 8:34 a.m.** When it's time to go separate ways, the most ephemeral items may attain iconic status, possession of which also signifies moral vindication. In the case of a soon-to-be-ex-couple on Sunset Avenue, it was food items in the icebox. She wanted them, he said no, and police paid a call, standing by as she gathered her belongings – possibly raiding the fridge one last time – and left.

**1:33 p.m.**
Out at the roundabout
The traffic made them have it out
Things didn't go their way
Call them ragers driving through the town and over to the cop shop
In and around the lot
Drivers come off of the road and yell there
Yes, just one more car-related road dispute
Two more drivers shouting who was rude to who
APD diplomacy becalmed the feud.

**7:32 p.m.** In a scheme worthy of *Mission Impossible,* a pizza fell into dastardly hands by means of a cunning ploy. Ordered by phone from an upper H Street address, a delivery guy showed up at an apartment which appeared vacant. Except, that is, for someone who snatched the pie and slammed the door. The delivery guy went and called police, who returned and found the apartment completely vacant. Logged as a grand theft.

**• Saturday, January 19 2:36 a.m.** There was someone with a gun at the donut bar, a cell phone caller told the CHP. When the call was transferred to APD, the line was dead. Nothing more dangerous than maple bars and crullers were located at the donut bar. The CHP reported that the cell phoner had been making "jokes and fake calls," and that they would be trying to track the caller down.

**2:18 p.m.** A woman said she'd been assaulted during an argument over a bag of cat food and a bucket of kitty litter. The case will be sent to the District Attorney for review.

**2:33 p.m.** A person erroneously reported staggering southbound in and out of traffic on one-way northbound G Street at 15th Street was actually looking for a poorly located wormhole in time and space – a pop-up portal to step into and be whisked away. Evidently he found it, for when police arrived, the staggerer had vanished.

**5:39 p.m.** A man called police from upper G Street saying he couldn't find his car. The call's purpose is unfathomable, since he wouldn't give his name, declined assistance and seemed very confused. But maybe his attention was elsewhere – an official at a nearby pornography emporium confirmed that the caller is a regular.

**6 p.m.** The frequent porner, still missing his car, was next reported wandering around inside a nearby art supply store. It wasn't there either.

**6:32 p.m.** The car searcher fell even further out of his porn orbit with a swoop through the Plaza. A new theory held that his son had the missing wheels, and police finally located the auto in the 1300 block of H Street.

**9:16 p.m.** Back up to the porn haven, where a different strange person was shriveling the business climate. Police entered; outcome undocumented.

• **Sunday, January 20 1:13 a.m**. Unbelievably, if what police say is true, an individual actually thought he could drink alcohol and drive a motor vehicle. Sounds dangerous – let's hope no one else ever tries this. First detected in the 800 block of Samoa Boulevard, the diluted driver was arrested in the 400 block of I Street on charges of driving schnockered; having an open hooch container; packing on his person not more than one avoirdupois ounce of marihoochie; and obstructing an officer.

**2:49 p.m.** A G Street caller reported a mercury spill in his home, with the liquid heavy metal flowing off his kitchen counter into the drain, and phones started ringing. APD contacted City water technicians, who referred the matter to the Eureka Fire Department's Hazardous Materials Unit. We don't do merc, they said, and bounced it back to Arcata's Environmental

Services department. The director there said he'd call Arcata's City Manager, who consulted with AVFD and called County HazMat. Finally, qualified personnel responded to the scene and collected the mercury. Mercury affects the human brain, spinal cord, kidneys and liver. It affects the ability to see, feel, taste and move. Long-term exposure causes progressively worse symptoms and may lead to personality changes, stupor and coma. Discarded thermometers account for an estimated 17 tons of mercury introduced into the environment annually.

**3:53 p.m.** It's not as if the dog found with no collar or tags materialized out of thin air. No, its appearance is a testament to the callous expediency of the unknown human who dumped it. The cast-off canine then entered the endgame of modern American pet processing, as in: If it isn't cute or convenient anymore it goes to the gas chamber.

**4:45 p.m.** Someone was reported "spinning brodies" in front of an L.K. Wood Boulevard residence, wrecking stuff up. Police will be visiting the area more frequently by night.

**6:50 p.m.** Lady, this is Arcata. Anything with any real, remote, perceived or imagined value left exposed and unattended, say in the back of a pickup truck for "just a second" is gone. Now you know.

**• Monday, January 21 2:17 a.m.** Contacted during a bicycle stop, a man was arrested on outstanding warrants and also charged with possession of a controlled substance and the dope-fiend technology required to ingest same.

**2:54 a.m.** Equipped with opposing thumb and forefinger, an ingrained hunter-gatherer species tradition and a crazy dream, a man entered a 24-hour supermarket, and, say police, stuffed some animal parts under his jacket and fled the store. But he and his ill-gotten meat were quickly corralled in the 100 block of F Street, and he (the suspect) was arrested and jailed on a burglary charge and escorted to the Pink House. *Yo, what're you in for?* Boosted a car. *You?* Knocked over a gas station. *You?* Flank steak in my flannel.

**12:28 p.m.** Deemed unfit for an F Street coffee temple, an obstreperous soul was ejected. Outside, he carried on in strident tones. Arcata Police, those ever-versatile civil servants, consulted with the screamer and made the place agreeable to those whose jitters are induced by caffeine and not a flailing nutcase.

**4:21 p.m.** Maybe, like humans, dogs too are just generally angrier these days. This time a golden lab with a less-than-golden 'tude was getting *grrr-y* with passing dogs being walked on proper leads. An officer talked to the owner, who secured the lab.

**7:22 p.m.** Arrest me, said the man at the police station. I'm wanted on a DUI warrant. He was, and they did.

**9:30 p.m.** The Earth is not your ashtray, and Redwood Park is not your campground.

• **Wednesday, January 23 4:08 a.m.** The sound of someone sitting. That's what a South G Street resident reported emanating from his porch. Police checked the area, and saw and heard nothing.

**5:08 a.m.** An hour later, same sit-uation.

**12:20 p.m.** Who needs a road? Parking lots are perfectly suitable rage-o-ramas. When someone speeds, spirited verbal exchanges follow, right when, in this case, a cop is passing by.

**5:02 p.m.** There was something dopey about that package, as Maggie, the happy little drug dog, verified at the Post Office. Narcotics investigation initiated.

**7:46 p.m.** Accounts differed so vastly – one claimed the other had tried to whap him with a crutch, while the other said the first one had tried to handcuff him – that nothing could really be done, and everyone just wanted to drop it.

• **Thursday, January 24 8:43 a.m.** Someone said someone was rude in Valley West.

**9:37 a.m.** Someone else said someone else was rude in Valley West.

**12:19 p.m.** A 4 lb. blue Topaz crystal was stolen the day before from a G Street purveyor of stones.

**12:29 p.m.** Motion sensors on Diamond Drive can't distinguish between evil intruders and family dogs.

**1:55 p.m.** The letters of warning over numerous outstanding violations were ignored, and so, the immobilizing boot went on the car in the 300 block of Laurel Drive.

• **Friday, January 25 1:55 a.m.** Those days of denial are over after the traffic stop in the 1000 block of Sixth Street. The two warrants paved a paper trail to jail.

**8:29 a.m.** If you saw a yellow and brown 1979 Mercury with no license plates and full of men and dogs parked outside your window, you'd surely feel the same sense of comfort and serenity that led a Fifth Streeter to dial APD. Police found the scuzzmobile and initiated a sprightly conversation which included topics like illegal camping, animal ordinances and trespassing.

**12:09 p.m.** The Grim Ranger harvested two more traveling souls from the 14th Street side of Redwood Park. Dope, of course.

**12:43 p.m.** No more mind-melding with a microchip now that the Playstation has been stolen from an Alliance Road address.

**3:06 p.m.** That I Street supermarket is cooperative, but not when it comes to pocketing unpaid-for groceries.

**3:31 p.m.** Seen arguing on Janes Road, their stories were as different as are men and women. He said their romance was on the rocks. She said he was a grabby stalker. Separate directions were charted for the two, and she was satisfied.

**3:53 p.m.** Some say there's drugs a-dealin' on Ross Street.

**6:42 p.m.** A Heather Lane resident opened her door only to be battered by an omelette/fusillade of eggs/verbal abuse. The alleged chef denied it.

• **Saturday, January 26 2:28 a.m.** Time to steer a couple tons of steel around City streets – think I'll consume excessive amounts of brain-scrambling elixir. Police took him from the 900 block of I Street to the Pink House.

**2:39 a.m.** Another booze-woozed driver in the 1600 block of 11th Street made an Arcata friend in Big Pink.

**5:17 a.m.** He was drunk, belligerent and wanted into the house. She, oddly enough, didn't want to admit him. Police relocated the chap to a steely remove.

**12:24 p.m.**
Four fans of the TH and C
Thought the park was a swell place to be
And smoke without danger
*Oh shit, there's the Ranger!*
Hi folks, may I see your I.D.?

**3:35 p.m.** The blue jacket and beanie made a stylish statement on the inside of the Ninth Street dumpster in which the bearded traveler was found. He was just passing through town and the dumpster, he said.

**5 p.m.**
He came in through a bathroom window
Sometime around the hour of noon
And who it was they have to wonder
'Cause her purse vanished from her room.
Didn't anybody catch him?
Didn't anybody see?
Now she's out a chunk of money
And on the phone to APD. Oh yeah.

**9:20 p.m.** A clothing shop at 11th and K seemed an unlikely place for a loud party, and there was a logical explanation. It was a dance/concert for a teen band, with clothes racks pushed out of the way to make room for the music. A noise warning was issued.

**10:04 p.m.** Let's go out to the closed boat basin where police will be immediately interested in us. I'll bring the dope, you bring the open container of hooch.

• **Sunday, January 27 1:42 p.m.** A driver on Alliance Road took her eyes off the road for a moment to tend to her kids, and the car swerved through a fence and into a yard. Passengers narrowly escaped serious injury when a large beam slammed straight in through the windshield.

**4:38 p.m.** Later, someone thought white road flare residue from the accident was something suspicious.

**4:59 p.m.** Sitting in the Pink House day after day, all he has to do is stew about that bad dope deal from a year ago. The only way to lash out is by phone, and according to a person who took a call from him, that's just what he did. A terrorist threat report was declined, but the incident was documented.

**6:36 p.m.**
Souls once joined
In crystalline completeness
Now jagged shards
That broken bowl
The messed-up dresser drawers
A bashed-in bedroom door
*Damn.*

• **Monday, January 28 1:43 p.m.** A youth was cited for having one of the following: a dirk, dagger, ice pick, knife having a blade longer than two-and-a-half inches, folding knife with a blade that locks into place, a razor with an unguarded blade, a taser, or a stun gun, an instrument that expels a metallic projectile such as a BB or a pellet, through the force of air pressure, CO2 pressure, or spring action, or any spot marker gun at the high school.

**3:01 p.m.** A hysterical call came in from Western Avenue, with the caller reporting that people all hopped up on marijuana and methamphetamine were going to try to run him over as he blocked their vehicle from leaving the scene. The line then went dead. Police found a more or less routine landlord/tenant dispute; not the dire druggie-drivey sitch earlier described.

**10:25 p.m.**
Wanted on warrants
He scrammed when he saw police
Chased down, cuffed; look – *pot!*

• **Tuesday, January 29 9 a.m.** A young man out on a sprainting spree, clad in a classic 21st Century hood uniform including the mandatory sweatshirt and identity-concealing hood, vandalized the Ninth and G phone booth and marked the PG&E box there. In this case, they actually snagged the little creepy crawly. Sure, he denied it at first, then admitted and erased the ugliness. Now he's on file and effectively neutered as a graffiti tagger.

**12:05 p.m.** Three men in Redwood Park set sail for the cosmos on wings of THC. But like Icarus, they flew too near the sun, or in this case the heat, in the person of Ranger Bob. Those citations were quite a bringdown.

**12:48 p.m.** A baby girl thought lost on South G Street was found in a truck in the garage. *Whew.*

**5:40 p.m.** "If you look in this direction at my daughter, you're gonna pay for it." This was the icebreaker one man offered another on Community Park Way, when he thought the guy'd been leering at his kid. Both men were counseled to stay away from each other.

**10:05 p.m.** An officer's just walking through that Janes Road pattern restaurant helped quell unruly tendencies by boisterous customers.

• **Wednesday, January 30 11:59 a.m**. If fashion could convict, the green hooded sweatshirt might have been probable cause. But the hood's companion, clad in arrest-me camouflage jacket and defiant red hat, would surely be jailbound. It was the drugs police say they found that sealed the probation violation and a trip to the Pink House.

**1:17 p.m.** Four travelers in Redwood Dog and Drug Park settled down for a picnic at the table near the 14th Street parking lot, and broke out their repast – a big fat reefer. The plot thickened – as did the picnickers' court files – when the Grim Ranger happened by.

**1:46 p.m.** Marijuana's popularity has spread even to that bastion of wholesomeness, the garbage-strewn, graffiti-splattered wasteland along the train tracks 'twixt the storage yard and the old lumber mill. There, two groups of eight or so leisure lurkers passed pipes, quaffed beers and maintained a perpetual state of near-total mental and physical debilitation while trading unverifiable anecdotes and folklore about how the Man is keeping them down. Police visited but found nothing amiss, which isn't surprising since the location features only two approaches along the train tracks, both of which afford a great and timely view of any approaching gendarmes.

**4:36 p.m.** Another call to the perpetual train track party, where a young runaway was located and turned over to county authorities.

**5:08 p.m.** Hockey players used the tennis courts in Larsen Park for more puckish pursuits, and when tennis players asked if they could use the courts as intended, there was an awful racket. Police found four young hockeyists, who agreed to leave.

**6:12 p.m.** A mom told a grown-up son that it was time he moved out and got a place of his own.

**8:49 p.m.** As a woman cleaned the interior of her car at a Valley West car wash, she noticed a guy in a gray Taurus circling, stopping and leering at her as she assumed the ungainly positions required for auto vacuuming, making her uncomfortable. Police were called, the oglemobile roared away.

• **Thursday, January 31 10:59 a.m.** It takes a frustrated soul to torment an answering machine with 14 harassing phone calls in one day.

**11:18 a.m.** A little dog wandered too near an electric fence on Old Arcata Road and... *zap!* The jolted pooch gradually recovered.

**3:42 p.m.** More new acquaintanceships between cops and embittered jolly-boys were forged at the train tracks.

• **Saturday, February 2 12:20 a.m.** For some reason, a

caller thought the sight of six bike riders wearing ski masks with no lights on their bicycles and heading towards a 24-hour mini-mart looked suspicious. Police cruised the area but found nothing of the stealthy swarm.

**12:40 p.m.** They could have sat down with carpentry tools and a hunk of wood and reinvented the wheel, but instead three travelin' men sparked up a doobie in Redwood Park within sight of a clear-eyed ranger.

**3:45 p.m.** What do pumpkins, corn stalks and underwear have in common? All served as handy hurling objects for college students on Western Avenue. The melange of random projectiles landed over the fence, on the property of a neighbor who found them inconsistent with the prevailing yard decor. The students weren't home and were to be contacted later.

**8:08 p.m.** An ad hoc wing-ding in the recessed entrance to the old shoe shop was temporarily wet-blanketed by police.

**9:03 p.m.** But just one visit couldn't quash the sheer jolliness at the little alcove, and another visit was required. Several sitabouts went passive till police left.

**10:13 p.m.** Like clockwork, the grungy little sidewalk tidepool again drew police interest. A spirited traveler was arrested and Pink-tanked.

**10:32 p.m.**
A Union Street bongo incursion
Led cops to a sudden immersion
In loud party fun
The host was told, "Son,
Better work out a quieter version."

**11:13 p.m.** Coupla kids nabbed some J.D. from a 24-hour supermarket and ran out. A security guard confronted the dashing duo outside. They ditched the whiskey and ran off.

**1:53 a.m.** Three liquored-up menfolk at an ampersanded Plaza tavern dragged their knuckles up off the floor, formed them into sweaty fists and aimed them unsteadily at each other. Bar closing time was just the beginning of their stay in the county tank.

**2:36 a.m.** Whatever rowdy pursuits those guys were involved in by the dumpster behind a Valley West budget motel, police kiboshed it.

**9:19 a.m.** Discerning Bayside Road auto burglars targeted high-qual Hondas and Toyotas. And then there was that Pontiac.

**12:52 p.m.** Ex-lovers crossed that thin line into yelling, threats and "That's it, I'm calling the police!" She just wanted the whole thing documented.

**3:11 p.m.** The steel incisors of a set of bolt cutters laughed their way through a wimpy bike chain on Union Street.

• **Monday, February 4 1:27 p.m.** A woman loaned her credit card to a friend for a $40 buy, and the now ex-friend ran up a $3,100 bill for whatever on the Internet. A payment arrangement was worked out, but the very ex-friend welched on the deal. Next, court.

**4:05 p.m.** Of all things, *threatening pieces of wood* came into a man's life at his workplace. The victim said another man was in cahoots with someone known only as "Don." One chunk of wood was inscribed with the message, *"To Don, maybe we should do a drive-by,"* and sent to the victim. No contact with the alleged wood senders was wanted; rather, the victim wanted the matter documented. He was to try to resolve things with his employer.

**4:30 p.m.** They didn't need Maggie the perky black lab to tell them that the package received for shipping at a Ninth Street hardware store was loaded with stinky stickybud, though little

Mags did confirm it.

• **Wednesday, February 6 9:04 a.m.** Two fun-lovin' souls, a redneck costume and a prop gun all drew police to an improvised movie set on 11th Street. When an officer arrived, the meta-redneck had morphed into a proto-pimp, and suffered a mock arrest.

**1:55 p.m.** The rain-sodden sofa was officially sighted over at the train track party. States the police bulletin, in dispatcherspeak: "Several unwanted subjects near tracks. Have furniture."

**4:15 p.m.** That nice green 21-speed on Austin Way is just a memory now.

**4:43 p.m.** Ditto the yellow boy's bike at the Community Pool.

**5:20 p.m.** The situation up on L.K. Wood Boulevard had deteriorated into yelling and swearing over the fence. Police brought what good cheer they could.

**5:58 p.m.** The Grand Marquis in the 600 block of 11th Street became a vinyl-lined sensory deprivation chamber for a dog locked inside with no food or water. Animal Control was on it.

**10:38 p.m.** "I'll slice you open," quipped a man to a liquor store operative who didn't wish to become a deli item on the Plaza. No knife was found, and the guy was advised not to return.

• **Thursday, February 7 2:20 a.m.** The blazing fluorescence of the 24-hour supermarket on F Street is like flame to a moth, as personified in this case by the man "carrying a guitar, garbage" there. He ran aground behind the laundromat, was cuffed and ushered away to the Pink House.

**6:30 p.m.** A 911 caller told the dispatcher she'd been sick, wouldn't say who she was and mumbled a lot. Police went to her home, as they must, and she blamed it on her ex, who was gone.

**8:37 p.m.** He said she showed up at his house, pushed him, kicked him in the leg and pulled the phone cord out of the wall. He just wanted police to know.

• **Friday, February 8 1:10 a.m.** The frequent camper from Hungary known as "Star Mind" fell to earth in the shadowy recesses of the Redwood Lounge.

**8:42 a.m.** Three tires on a forklift were punctured in the night by anti-forklift guerillas on Golf Course Road.

**3:38 p.m.** Spillover youth energy from the Skate Park formed a frolicsome frisson of fisticuffs at nearby Larsen Park, where lads in headgear and gloves took to boxing. Some 50 to 60 high school kids watched the fight club, then dispersed.

**9:17 p.m.** A number of loud party complaints rolled in from the Sunset area. Police provided poopage.

**11:58 p.m.** It first appeared to be a bucket of little liquor bottles which the hooded figure had stolen from a Northtown market, running off on the slogan-slathered footbridge over the freeway. But the store called back saying only bubble gum had been taken, and never mind.

• **Saturday, February 9 8:05 a.m.** A large black lab running in and out of traffic and into a downtown coffee temple in search of its human was taken into custody and lodged in the City holding pen.

**10:50 a.m.** An embattled laundromat in Sunny Brae – victim of a daring rooftop-entry heist a few years back – was again shaken down for its treasure of quarters, when someone used a screwdriver to force open washing machine coin boxes.

**11:38 a.m.** Star Mind was again corralled in Redwood Park and was taken into custody by Immigration and Naturalization Service authorities for possible return to his native nebula.

**6:10 p.m.** *Oh, bad guys:* an A Street resident would like their power drill and bicycle back.

**8:05 p.m.** A mean little cuss – short, with no front teeth and of course wearing the mandatory baseball cap – positioned himself on the porch of a Northtown coffee house and tried to start fights with customers. But instead of symbolically filling the gap in his teeth and life by reaping the joys of conquest, he was instead hauled off by cops on an outstanding warrant and probation violation. He and his issues went to the Pink House.

**9:42 p.m.** Motor running on the car parked crossways at the entrance to the darkened CHP station, door open and warning tone bleating wanly beneath her cries for help as she pounded on the front door – to no avail, since the office isn't staffed after hours. Back to her car and on the cell phone to her brother with a panicked tale of a boyfriend following and harassing her. Brother to APD: she's on her way over. Police met her in the parking lot, and soon the boyfriend was en route to Big Pink, charged with assault on a cohabitant.

**11:54 p.m.** Leaving his sweet girl dog outside a Plaza liquor store just long enough to pop in for a refreshment, he emerged to find her gone. DJ is about 30 lbs., black and brown with a distinctive wrinkly forehead and unmistakable white front leg (the owner declined to specify left or right), and something of a one-mutt melting pot of breeds – a Shar-pei/Rhodesian ridgeback/black lab mix. The dognapper is described as a guy in a reggae hat, whatever that is, who was "trying to impress two girls" by the sure-fire method of stealing a loose dog outside a liquor store. Darren misses his companion, and asks that anyone who knows where DJ is call him at the Arcata Endeavor or catch up with him on the train tracks by the storage yard.

• **Sunday, February 10 12:57 a.m.** With every step down H Street, a fresh curse departed his lips at not insignificant volume. In a startling development, alcohol was involved. Off to the county tank.

**3:50 a.m.** You wouldn't answer a knock on your door either, if the person knocking wouldn't say anything when you asked who was there. More bibulous bilge for the drunk tank.

**8:57 a.m.** A lot of fun was had at the big party on Curtis Way the previous night, much of it to be found in the form of spent beverage husks discarded in the street there and on Forest Avenue. A hostess blearily agreed to clean up the mess.

• **Sunday, February 11 2:28 p.m.** The Breakfast Club's old haunt at the Marsh is all but unusable, now that the anti-boozer ordinance is in effect there and their little grassy cul-de-sac has been trimmed back, The train tracks by the old mill serve these days as a semi-isolated tidepool for tipplers and tokers. The good part is, you can see anyone coming a good ways off. The bad part is, anyone can see you going a good ways off. That is, should one wish to piddle, diddle, dally or otherwise generate jollies with a consenting member of the opposite configuration, you need to find a secluded space – *fast!* And so it was that a he and she were greeted in a yard near Eighth and N streets. They skedaddled on officers' request, afterglow forfeited.

**3:15 p.m.** We checked with Satan himself on this one, and it's true – a special level of Hell exists for anyone who would graffiti a Victorian home. By doing so, one chap has made his reservation.

**4:53 p.m.** That neighbor-against-neighbor situation in the 2300/2400 block of L.K. Wood Boulevard has borne its inevitable fruit – a restraining order.

**7:32 p.m.** Ostensibly, it was about one roommate knocking over a shelf in the other's room. At least that was the trigger.

The real deal was money and bills. A bloody nose, and contused head, a bunch of cops and both parties declined prosecution.

• **Monday, February 12 12:46 a.m.** That pool ball must have symbolized life itself, so dearly did the probationer cling to it outside the Plaza sports bar. Efforts to repatriate the ball to the mother ship met with bared teeth and arrayed knuckles, and police were summoned. Soon the Keeper of the Orb was stretched out on a Pink House cot, bearing one less ball than he wished.

**2:32 a.m.** Those who occupy the high-density residential inn on Union Street make their own fun, out of whatever may be available. So if "beating on floors" is the way some there choose to pass the wee hours, only their fellow tenant downstairs is in a position to complain. Which he did.

**1:53 p.m.** Three travelers in Redwood Park weren't quite happy enough without The Drug. The Park Ranger cited them, essentially for smoking without a license.

**3:33 p.m.** A woman allegedly switched price tags on a couple of items – presumably placing a lower price on the merch she wanted, which happened to be a set of waders. Her filching expedition earned her a stay in the Pink House on charges of petty theft and probation violation.

**5:39 p.m.** A baker's dozen of smot pokers inhaled magical vapours along the tracks, getting, well, baked. When police arrived, their numbers had, like her eyelids, dropped by half, leaving only a half dozen or so amiable souls.

• **Wednesday, February 13 12:17 a.m.** He wore dark clothing, she said, and chased her right up to her doorstep wailing about "Arcata taking his dog." Compelling as the approach was, she didn't wish to be a stand-in for the errant mutt. The guy's friends say that, bereaved or not, he's become quite the tedious pain in the ass, always wingeing on about his missing dog, and maybe fate is trying to tell him that he just wasn't meant to have one.

**6:26 a.m.** An HSU student must have a pretty low opinion of the literacy of the people who empty the recycling bin in Valley West, into which he dumped a bunch of his old tests, magazines and nonrecyclable garbage. In fact, they could read, his gamble didn't pay, and he was soon scrounging the crud out of the bin.

**12:49 p.m.** A tenant complained about conditions in the bathroom, and the landlord came over for a little argument. Actually a big one, in which he blocked the door and wouldn't leave. Eventually, he did.

**1:15 p.m.**
Take me out at the Ball Park
Take my stash away there
Cite me for reefer and search my pack
Tell me I ought to never come back
...And it's one, two, three hits you're out of the old Ball Park.

**1:57 p.m.** A theft of merchandise at an I Street cooperative supermarket was followed by a foot chase by employees and a petty theft charge against an individual. The coveted item? A can of Budweiser.

**• Thursday, February 14 12:51 a.m.** Counterintuitively, beating on the door, threatening residents and refusing to leave an Olympia Street address is not the best way to ingratiate oneself into others' good graces.

**1:29–2:06 p.m.** Redwood Park users learned that there's more to having a dog than feeding it and letting it run loose any old where. Things like licenses and leashes are part of the reality. But maybe they too just aren't up to dogship.

**3:27 a.m.** Trespassers were found inside the hot tub area at the Community Pool. One used a false name which police somehow found less than credible: "Jerry Butcheg."

**8:45 a.m.** A traveler was observed emptying trash from the cans on the Plaza, possibly as a very low-budget Feng Shui project. An officer stopped and asked him to put it all back, and while he was reluctant to do so, he complied.

**6:05 p.m.** People were reported using a porta-potty with the door open, and playing loud music on Samoa Boulevard. Police contacted four people, who agreed to turn down the music. Closing the dang door may be a future aspiration.

**7:03 p.m.** A car with its lights off pulled into the lower I Street Marsh parking lot and drove recklessly all around it. A man said he was teaching his sister how to drive, and that braking practice was the subject of that night's lesson.

**8:09 p.m.** Someone called APD "raving" about being upset with APD about not arresting enough criminals. An officer went out to see if the caller might qualify to help raise the average, but the complainant wasn't nutto enough to commit.

**• Saturday, February 16 8:30 a.m.**
A traveler at the bus station
Had paused in his earthly migrations
To stop and play house
Till cops came to roust
And wrote him a camping citation.

**9:34 a.m.**
A traveler, dog on the loose
Was Marshing, without an excuse
There, poodle or beagle
Loose dogs are illegal
So wildlife won't get abuse.

**10:52 a.m.** More al fresco funsters made a new blue friend in Redwood Park.

**12:14 p.m.**
And speaking of Redwood Park frolic
A brace of marijuanaholics
Were written citations
In Cannabis Nation
Where punishment's largely symbolic.

**12:26 p.m.** A Valley West home of honest goodness became, police allege, a nest of dishonest badness as several subjects were contacted regarding a flinky check someone was trying to pass at the video counter. One man fled and was chased on foot, with HSU Police assisting APD in the matter.

**12:41 p.m.**
Flash back to the Redwood Park meadow
Where a reefer *aficionedo*
Was nabbed in a thicket
Then given a ticket
And wandered off somewhat unsteado.

**Gutted and discarded in downtown alleys.**

**8:41 p.m.** Arcata's famed liberal tolerance does not extend to politically conservative lawn signs on B Street, which were sundered by forces of enlightenment under cover of darkness.

**8:55 p.m.** No, it only *sounds* like skateboarders are bustin' things up behind a Westwood Center market.

• **Sunday, February 17, 12:25 a.m.** So very whacked out was this guy that it took two police forces – UPD and APD – to quell his furies. Which they did.

**8:48 a.m.**
A big black cow, loose
On Samoa Boulevard
Somehow got away.

**2:22 p.m.** "You're lucky I haven't hurt you yet." That cheery felicitation, allegedly offered by an ex-boyfriend at a Sunny Brae supermarket, led to a phone call to APD.

**3:15 p.m.** About 10 dogs were reported running loose in Redwood Park, but when police arrived, they were all under human control. Until police left.

**6:15 p.m.** Someone called from the hospital, claiming a driver's side mirror had been sheared off while the car was parked at the ER. An officer deemed this account dubious, mostly due to the cobwebs which had already formed on the aging remnants of the busted mirror.

• **Monday, February 18 1:06 p.m.** A man asked police to make his girlfriend stop hitting him. But when an officer arrived, the two were negotiating calmly.

**3:43 p.m.** A man came to APD claiming that he'd been improperly evicted from his rental property, and call the landlord. The lord said the place had been declared a public nuisance, because it wasn't actually designed for human habitation. The guy finished moving out, which is probably just as well, since he says he constantly smelled natural gas there.

• **Tuesday, February 19 2:50 p.m.** She said the harasso-calls had been coming for six months from... *beep!* Hold on, I have another call. It was the alleged harasser. Police issued a warning.

**5:30 p.m.** A woman reported that someone uncovered her vehicle, stole it and drove it exactly eight miles, then returned it. The proof was that her odometer had changed from 70 to 78. When an officer met with her, she explained how a magnetic force from space was harassing her. Police stepped up patrols.

• **Thursday, February 21 12:43 p.m.** Police waded into the daily gathering of the Fun Bunch out by the train tracks, where four travelers went through some official rigamarole culminating in issuance of citations for undisclosed Muni Code violations.

**5:24 p.m.** Someone reported having bought a car from a person who was now threatening to "blow up" the vehicle, and that wasn't part of the original deal. Police advised the two to take it to court.

**10:50 p.m.** Dude was so wiped he was passed out on Haeger Avenue – literally. Someone trained their headlights on the sodden figure so he wouldn't get run over. Somehow verticality was achieved, and a clearheaded person walked the speed bump home.

• **Friday, February 22 2:10 a.m.** A man peed all over some shopping carts in an F Street parking lot, then got in a blue car with three others and zoomed.

**4:39 p.m.** Those Nigerian-origin scam letters must work on somebody, since they keep appearing.

**6:18 p.m.** A Heather Lane resident alleged that someone had left the hose running just to run up his water bill. But an officer found someone washing a car and no excessive water used.

**10:21 p.m.** A technoblivious prankster making prank calls in the Age of Caller I.D. is bound to hear from police.

**• Saturday, February 23 12:11 a.m.**
Red Toyota truck
Trying to ram someone else
One more drunk driver.

**• Saturday, February 23 1:14 a.m.** A traveler bunked down for a night's sleep in the doorway of a Northtown porn citadel, and drunkenly resisted suggestions that he depart the well-traveled gateway to xxxstacy. An officer lured him into a cell.

**1:50 a.m.**
When most folks were home in their beds
A tavern well-stocked with stuffed heads
Had drunks at its doors
Cops scooped up the boors
(And) installed them in jail instead.

**5:31 a.m.** It wasn't necessarily remarkable that a man relieved bladder pressure in the pre-dawn darkness of Heindon Road, only a little puzzling, since a 24-hour diner complete with a modern indoor water closet beckoned just an urgent walk away. Most noteworthy was that, as the pungent urinary vapors swirled up from the pavement, commingling with morning mists of the nearby compromised wetland and tangy hydrocarbon exhaust wafting over from the freeway, someone saw the leaky chap greeting the dawn with his streaming salutation and called police. The call mandated a flashing-light rendezvous at the man's next destination, a gas station across the freeway. He admitted the illicit drainage and agreed to confine his emissions to an appropriate – and private – venue in the future.

• **Sunday, February 24 12:25 a.m.** They weren't The Who, they just played them in a Valley West motel room. Asked to leave room 228, a torrid twosome instead reportedly applied their energies to destroying it. Police were more persuasive in engineering a departure, and the kids were all right.

**1:14 a.m.** The timeless Battle of the Sexes took a tacky turn on Hallen Drive, where a bruising brawl was reported in Apartment A. Police found a man sitting in a car outside, with her still inside behind closed doors. Horseplay had gotten out of control, it was explained. Just a friendly dispute among consenting horseplayers.

**1:31 a.m.** A twosome out in Valley West weren't to be outdone for *film noir* abstrusion. She was said to be passed out in the bike lane by a gas station. When police arrived, she had apparently made her way over to a nearby veterinary clinic, and a male was seen bending over her. Those on scene were "trying to figure out what to do." Desperate as the situation sounds, it was decided that no further assistance was needed, so there's obviously more to the situation than was documented.

**1:59 p.m.** Skateboarding at an A Street church, dog running loose... for a brief time, it was as though they alone occupied the Earth, with no one else's well-being to consider and no social contract to heed. Until the law arrived with warnings and citations.

**4:47 p.m.** Police aren't a taxi service, but public safety is what they're all about. So when the caretaker of a 93-year-old man locked her keys in the car at the Post Office, of course she was given a quick ride home to pick up an extra key so the elderly gentleman wouldn't have to be alone too long.

**8:28 p.m.** A male-type person in the 1000 block of G Street acted out behaviors more or less characteristic of that gender, which included screaming and pounding the ground. Since he didn't hold elected office and wasn't seeking one, the behavior was deemed irrational – some people actually reversed direction rather than enter his jurisdiction. Arcata Police were busy elsewhere, and an HSU officer checked it out. The screamer had pounded a path away from the scene.

**11:18 p.m.** Yelling off a balcony in the 100 block of Samoa Boulevard just wasn't enough – a trumpet solo augmented the mix. Again, police found no one there.

**• Monday, February 25 3:05 p.m.** Thirsty sleazeballs ripped off working people by taking a 12-pack from a Valley West liquor store without paying anything for the watery grog. The sleazemobile they raced away in was your basic piece of shit clapped-out old Nissan, an undifferentiated light blue or silver in sleazy hue.

**3:06 p.m.** For not the first time, someone phoned worried about the figure lying on the ground at Seventh and A streets. Johnny was just catching some rays.

**3:53 p.m.** Her ex admitted entering her apartment through the unlocked rear sliding door, snagging her car keys and driving off in her van. He claimed they had an understanding that he could borrow the vehicle. *Uh-uh,* she said. He was told he had trespassed and that their ameliorated relationship was a no-borrow zone till further notice.

**• Thursday, February 28 5:53 p.m.** Someone trying to exchange $30–$40 worth of quarters on Valley East Boulevard aroused suspicion, what with all the washing machine break-ins. But she'd acquired the coins performing what may be the world's most unassailable wholesome and innocent activity – selling candy at a school fundraiser.

**6:43 p.m.** Someone kicked out of a minor H Street movie

theatre howled with anguish across the street for a time.

**9:47 p.m.** They'd never have been asked to leave Room 102 at a Northtown motel had they not played their so-called music that loud.

**11:13 p.m.** Motel abuse continued with party animals again rockin' Room 218 in Valley West.

**• Saturday, March 2 12:10 a.m.** Be my friend and resource – or else. This was the basic proposition of a man who called a woman asking to borrow her car. She declined, and was then told someone would be coming over to beat her up, break her windows and slash her tires. Since that's what friends aren't for, police called the man who said he had been angry, wasn't anymore, wasn't going to wreck her stuff and would apologize.

**2:08 a.m.** Numerous cocktail-imbued souls piled loudly into cars on Shirley Boulevard, leaving the party in a maelstrom of slammed doors, roaring engines and discarded drink canisters hitting the pavement after one last guzzle. "The car ran over my foot!" quipped one celebrant to the whole neighborhood.

**6:37 a.m.** Someone reported a loud band at Fifth and E streets, but it was one of those young men's obnoxiomobiles that thunder with bass as surrogate sonic plumage. The vehicle was parked and running with the driver passed out behind the wheel. He was awakened and sent inside.

**8:43 a.m.** Still more motel misadventure, with a party infestation in Room 114 at a Northtown motel. Police dispersed the sunrise soiree, with one attendee jailed on a public drunkenness charge.

**12:33 p.m.** Two youths stole some spray paint from a Sixth Street color center and took off running westbound as fast as their legs could carry them. They weren't found, but the paint will soon appear on a public wall near you.

**1:34 p.m.** Two menfolk were seen rearranging each others' faces in the 400 block of Samoa Boulevard. As police descended, one doddered away on drunken feet. The rest of him being in a similar state, police whisked him out of harm's way to the Pink House.

**6:43 p.m.** There was something suspicious about the traveler using a hose on M Street. Maybe it was the green food coloring he'd covered himself in from head to toe. He told an officer he'd woken up that morning and decided he'd be green that day "just because." He'd become concerned about a dry flower he noticed over the past few days, being a community-spirited sort, and green, decided to water it.

**• Sunday, March 3 12:55 a.m.** The Plaza's mad social whirl spiraled into recreational violence, with four or five gladiators fighting in the side alley. The actual conflict was traced to a third drinkery, and was found not to be physical, though surely not especially intellectual either.

**6:26 p.m.**
Three trav'lers who cleared vegetation
Had prepped a Marsh camp habitation
Cops came down with rules
And took cutting tools
For safekeeping back at the station.

**• Monday, March 4 11:48 p.m.** A big, goofy faux promotional bowling pin was spirited from the lobby of an historic Plaza storehouse and grafted to the hand of a Plaza presidential statue, which has previously sported protest signs, pot leaves and a stuffed rooster, among other non sequitur items. The crepe paper appendage remained in place for hours, barely impinging on the Stolid One's dignity. Rather, it only served to cement his rep as Arcata's one true kingpin.

**1:27 p.m.** Following her around and leaving notes at his ex-girlfriend's work inexplicably did not produce the fervently desired kissy-face scenarios. It's time for someone to sit down with Mr. Retroactively Smitten and give him the "she's not the only fish in the sea" talk.

**3:49 p.m.** A woman's purse was stolen right out of her Union Street home, and the bad guys are running up bills on her plastic.

**4:13 p.m.** Police held consultations with representatives of the Fun Bunch out on the tracks by the storage yard. One man with a bag of vegetable matter of a type his mother never urged him to consume, plus a warrant, won some Pink House hours.

**7:20 p.m.** A traveler hung out at the entrance/exit of an I Street cooperative supermarket, subjecting shoppers to his trip. Asked to leave, he and his lifestyle moved along.

**8:23 p.m.** Well, alcohol's pretty much shattered this guy's life. It didn't make his evening's lodging especially pleasant either.

**9:53 p.m.** A spray of granulated safety glass across the parking lot, empty space in her car where the CDs had been and a furtive figure wearing the mandatory baseball cap moving with dispatch north on Union Street.

**10:26 p.m.** A man complained that a former employee was removing property from his truck which the former employer owned, but that he was "assaulting" the truck while doing so. An officer stood by for the property transfer, and no one was mean to the truck.

**• Wednesday, March 6 1:04 a.m.** Camping at the Marsh isn't legal or eco-cool, nor conducive to a good night's sleep, as three travelers learned.

**1:43 p.m.** The Park Ranger dismantled a hobbit hollow in

Redwood Park.

**1:44 p.m.** A man walked into a 10th Street medical clinic and announced that he was going to do something "drastic." When police arrived, the reporting party declined further action.

**2:11 p.m.** How big a jerk do you hafta be to get kicked out of a highly tolerant, liberally indulgent and caffeine-effulgent downtown coffee temple?

**4:45 p.m.** A pedestrian was chased by one of Arcata's tens of millions of unleashed dogs, this one a yellowish lab, in the 1300 block of Sunset Avenue.

**9:17 p.m.** Someone reported taking "inappropriate" photos with a friend. The man who was to process the shots was asking for $500 or he would tell the photo subject's parents about the photos. If she goes to the police, he reportedly said, he'd post the photos on the Internet. The caller declined to file a report, but the incident was documented.

**9:26 p.m.** How much of a freak do you hafta be to get cop-extracted from a highly tolerant, etc., I Street cooperative supermarket?

**• Friday, March 8 12:17 a.m.** Police couldn't help but notice a man standing outside a Plaza sports bar pressing a towel to his head. He'd been cranium-bonked with a bottle, but didn't want to make a report, and declined assistance.

**1:37 p.m.** A suspected chicken-hungry dog was rounded up.

**• Saturday, March 9 12:19 a.m.** It was a night to remember – for all the wrong reasons. An 11th Street party ended with public drunkenness citations and underage kids given dread-filled rides home.

**10:43 p.m.** A drinker utilized a resident's porch in the 900 block of I Street as an imbibing station, and wouldn't leave until police were headed there.

**1:57 p.m.**
In the redwoods, Arcata's own ranger
Called for backup to minimize danger
While busting two fellers
He deemed reefer sellers
Who spent that night bunking with strangers.

• **Sunday, March 10 12:57 a.m.** When you stay at an historic Plaza hotel, you have to expect some sonic spillover from the vibrant town square, expressed as blood-curdling yelling and revving car engines. Maybe those new double-pane windows will help.

**1:18 p.m.** At Fun Bunch World Headquarters out on the train tracks past Bud's Mini-Storage, a far, far different type of "bud" was also available. Cited and released.

**7:10 p.m.** A traveling alcohol victim was transplanted from an H Street doorway to the slammer.

• **Monday, March 11 10:11 a.m.** Same guy, possibly tokin' de oib and refusing to leave the front of an I Street cooperative supermarket. Same result.

**11:02 a.m.** A Haeger Avenue resident was reported "tapping into cordless phone traffic." Reassuringly, the fellow scrutinizing others' conversations is said to live alone with his gun.

**11:29 a.m.** The previously documented obstinator had doubled back to the ITF/Endeavor area and had added snappy patter to his doings. After yelling at staff, he was warned and left.

**12:24 p.m.** It's not clear what utility a magnetic car door sign that says "Northcoast Adventures Kayaking" would have to anyone but the company, but since it was stealable, it was stolen.

**2:01 p.m.** The Weed Whacker Fairy came to the 100 block of Samoa Boulevard, broke into a locked shed and took away the device, but forgot to leave a quarter.

**4:21 p.m.** Rude-ass skate punks mouthed off near Ninth and H. One was arrested on a warrant and wheeled over to jail.

• **Tuesday, March 12 1:58 a.m.** In denial as to the hour, a couple of drunks tried with all their woozy might and main to penetrate the front door and window to a Plaza sports bar. Stymied by the fiendish wiles of the inanimate objects, the plastered pair were popped, then Pink-plunked.

**4:59 a.m.** A thin-faced man in his 20s fell out of his seat at a golden-arched Valley West fast food franchise restaurant, was acting strangely and couldn't communicate. Police found him at an area tire shop, where he had trouble speaking. It wasn't that his heart-stopping cuisine had taken its inevitable toll – yet. He had overmedicated.

**10:03 a.m.** A flasher made a great case for willful amnesia, showing someone parts of himself they would rather not have seen in the bushes in the 600 block of F Street. He got away.

• **Wednesday, March 13 7:09 a.m.**
A red Thunderbird sat alone
In Alliance Road's handicapped zone
It wasn't permitted
Its owner emitted
A three hundred-thirty buck moan.

**11:16 a.m.** This traveler wasn't a drunk, he just plays one in doorways.

**1:47 p.m.** Moron prints appeared on L Street storage units. An officer duly photographed the graffiti for the database.

**4:44 p.m.** A man in a blue 1991 Ford Escort perhaps understandably insisted that someone "trade cars" with him in a Valley West parking lot. The offer was declined.

• **Thursday, March 14 3:47 p.m.** Drunks bothered docs in the ER.

**7 p.m.** Pete was not wanted at a Sunset Avenue address. He was just trying to keep the good times rolling, and he loves you.

• **Sunday, March 17 12:13 a.m.** Two teenagers ripped off 24-ounce bottles of beer, one each, from an 11th Street supermarket and ran as fast as their legs could carry them south on Janes Road. Hearts pounding in triumph, they guzzled the illicit beverage from an unknown hidey-hole as an APD cruiser futilely roamed the streets looking for them.

**3:47 p.m.** Fuzzies congregated outside a Ninth Street hardware store, which bothered some customers. The hangabouts agreed to scoot.

• **Monday, March 18 1:17 p.m.**
At Ninth and H, somewhat uncooly
Four travelers acted unruly
When lippy ones hectored
The hippies were lectured
And left amid clouds of patchouli.

• **Tuesday, March 19 1:32 p.m.** The previously delightful planters outside a Ninth Street hardware store have gradually been chipped away by idlers.

**4:20 p.m.** At the most wonderful moment of the day, an officer appeared at Fun Bunch World HQ for frank and temporarily productive discussions.

**5:12 p.m.** Police performed a civil standby at an 18th Street house of Chi.

**11:24 p.m.** Three puffy-jacketed males went on a kind of mini-rampage in the 800 block of 12th Street. First, they downed a flimsy breakaway stop sign, which obediently broke away. Next, the fearless gladiators pulled a car's door handle. But even this accomplishment left their lust for conquest somehow unquenched, so one petulant puffy boy reportedly kicked the car. Police swarmed the site, charging two with possession of alcohol and vandalism.

• **Wednesday, March 20 3:03 p.m.** A man positioned himself in front of a Plaza liquor store and started yelling about women's breasts. An officer changed the subject.

**3:12 p.m.** A different report came in about the same man, who was reported using religious-themed obscenities on passersby, including unkind comments about a woman's sexual characteristics which her husband found most ungracious.

**3:24 p.m.**
Loose bovines were up to no good
On Samoa, where five of them stood
They chose to cavort
Near a basketball court
Till led back to planned burgerhood.

**5:57 p.m.** Steve-o's post-post-post-post-punk anarcho-metal bass guitar stylings simultaneously distressed, delighted and deafened music aficionados within an eighth-mile or so blast radius of Crescent Way and Bayside Road, which is probably just what he had in mind.

• **Saturday, March 23 9:35 a.m.** Anti-vacuum cleaner forces took direct action at the car wash on K Street, liberating oppressed auto sweepings from their canister bastilles and spreading same around the lot. Police will be seen in the area more frequently.

**11:58 a.m.** When he rented the videotapes, it was, implicitly, for a finite period of time sufficient to assimilate the *quality entertainment* magnetically encoded thereon. But the store hasn't seen them since, and letters are being returned as undeliverable.

**5:12 p.m.** A McKinleyville man walked into a Northtown bicycle shop and said he was "just looking." Moments later, the browser was heard, then seen roughly muscling a hyperexpensive "Kona Stinky" mountain bicycle out of a dense thicket of similar bikes on display. "It was as though the bike he was trying to free had had a premonition and did not want to leave its happy perch," recalled a store employee. "Don' worry, I ain't gonna hurt 'em," said the McKinleyviller, and with that, the bike popped free.

Though his appearance indicated that he might be something short of a tycoon, the McKinleyviller had selected a $1,700 bike, and without even a test ride, produced a credit card and he said he'd take it.

Store personnel were suspicious, especially when the McKinleyviller asked how much credit was available on the card but didn't want to call the credit card company. Still, the transaction went through, credit approval was gained without a hitch and the man was given back the card. An employee then took the bike in back for a standard, last-minute safety check, even though the customer wanted to leave with the bike. Fortunately, the McKineyviller needed a smoke and stepped outside, giving the employees a few minutes to think.

Though they might have let him go, the employees just didn't feel right about the sale and wanted to re-check the card. But they were torn. If they asked for the card back, a legitimate if unlikely customer might take offense and demand a refund, losing the store a substantial sale. But if, against their retail instincts, they released the bike and the transaction later turned out to be improper, then they'd be kicking themselves for having been had. So, one employee undertook some "last-minute faux repair work," while the other asked for the card, justifying it on the pretense that the authorization code which had been given was comprised only of numbers, not the usual letters and numbers.

After a mild protest, the McKinleyviller handed back the card and followed the worker back into the store. The employee pretended to swipe the card again, and punched the terminal's buttons "for beepy sound effects," then called the credit center to determine whether the card was stolen. And again, it was cleared for purchase.

Absolved of responsibility, an employee gave the McKinleyviller a last form to fill out, one for inventory and tax purposes. Then the strangeness returned, as the man asked what Arcata's zip code was and misspelled his last name. At this point, recalled an employee, "It is so wrong we can practically smell it." They told the man they had to tune the bike's suspension, suggested he go grab some coffee and come back, and he left the store.

Again an employee got on the phone, and just as the credit center operator assured him for the third time that all was well with the card, the other line rang. On it was an "angry, urgent voice" asking, "Did someone just buy a $1,700 bike at your shop?" It was the cardholder, who'd lost his plastic at a gas station the previous night and had just been told by the credit firm about the sale. "I'm calling the police – they'll be there in minutes!" he said.

Noted an employee, "The McKinleyvillian wrecked our Chi."

Arcata Police officers arrived, but were told that if the McKinleyviller saw them, he'd likely bail, so they "hovered" some distance away, according an officer. Shortly, the McK man returned for the final act.

An employee dialed 911, and the dispatcher said officers were five blocks out and closing. Employees tried to time the bike handoff so that the coming confrontation with police didn't take place inside the tight confines of the store, though they didn't want the McKinleyviller outside too soon so that he might see the cops coming from a long way off and run for it.

After some last-minute shilly-shallying, employee, customer and bike walk outside and come face to face with the law.

"Arcata Police. Can I see some ID, please?"

At that, the man turned around backward with his hands behind him in a quasi-humorous, "you got me" sort of mock-handcuffing pose.

"Uh, I don't have it with me," the McKinleyviller then

said as another police car arrived. The officer asked him to turn around in order to see if the man had a wallet on him, and reached out for his hand. But as soon as their hands made contact, the man screeched "Nooooo!" – "like a five year old," an employee later said. With that, the man dashed past the officer, who grabbed his shirt to try and knock him off balance, but couldn't get a grip.

The chase was on. The suspect ran around the back of the building and hopped a fence. Officers followed in pursuit, while an employee headed off around the block to intercept the man farther down the way. An officer managed to shoot a glancing spritz of pepper spray on the suspect's face, but not enough to stop him. Two officers ran through the stinging mist, causing slight discomfort.

Two blocks away, a store employee caught up with the man, who fell face down on a muddy slope. Police arrived within seconds, encircled him and took the man, who was swearing and his pants falling down, into custody.

Daniel Eugene Christie of McKinleyville was booked into the Humboldt County Correctional Facility on charges of burglary, fraudulent use of a credit card, possession of stolen property, forgery, resisting arrest and probation violation.

Christie reportedly told officers he'd tossed the credit card out his car window on Alliance Road, but it was never found. The theft victim's wallet was located inside Christie's vehicle.

Though two officers received minor hand injuries during the chase, one later said that "I had a great day – we caught the guy."

• **Sunday, March 24 1:14 a.m.** Plaza hotel lodgers complained of loud partyers out front, but technically they weren't out front, they were in front of the sports bar next door, and that made all the difference. Indeed, screaming drunks represent a cherished thread in Arcata's vibrant cultural tapestry.

**1:54 a.m.** That tapestry may have been a little threadbare just down a way, where a heartbroken would-be patron, in the throes of regret over what might have been in terms of unguzzled refreshments, kicked at the door of another tavern after it closed its doors for the night.

**1:09 – 2:44 p.m.** One doesn't normally consider Spear Avenue a roiling cauldron of antagonism, but beneath that deceptively placid exterior... First, someone drove across someone's lawn in the 3200 block, then someone else broke someone else's garage window. Neither act was apparently committed in a spirit of altruism.

**4:31 p.m.** A doggie-derived showdown on Wisteria Way, where an unleashed pooch pitted neighbors against each other. It poops in neighbors' yards, a man complained, and when he told the owner, she reportedly took a swing at him, knocking his hat off. She later admitted that her dogs ran onto his lawn, but claimed that he had had his dogs attack her dogs, and that was what started the argument. The humans agreed to just stay away from each other; the dogs gazed at the antics of the respective god-like masters with unquestioning love and devotion.

**9:30 p.m.** Neighbors' tolerance is wearing thin over the folks living in the van with their dogs at Sunset and Western avenues.

• **Monday, March 25 8:57 p.m.** A light bulb was left unscrewed at an Alliance Road apartment porch, and a suspect was named.

**10:29 p.m.** On upper G Street the mirth and merriment was unrestrained, and included loud music and talk, plus some giddy wall-pounding.

**11:20 p.m.** An I Street drummer chose this hour to exact torrid thumpery on neighbors.

• **Tuesday, March 26, 1:27 p.m.** Sidewalk socialites outside a downtown hardware store daily ask those passing by to support them. Some people are not fond of being importuned.

**4:02 p.m.** An officer roved down the rusty rails to meet with representatives of the Fun Bunch, whose so-called "fun" apparently revolves around untucked shirts, unpressed trousers, unruly sideburns, garish, impractical keychains, excessive salty snacks in lieu of fresh vegetables and brash, "rock-style" music played on jangling electrified guitars and wild tambourines.

**4:23 p.m.** A hardware store employee and a traveler had a spat in an alley; everyone survived to glare again at each other another day.

**4:51 p.m.** In case you wonder whether these items are fabricated, here's incontestible proof of their authenticity: No mortal could conjure the existence of a blue cooler full of Vaseline and hair ties abandoned on the side of West End Road.

**• Friday, March 29 1:54 a.m.** It's not clear what his plan was, the man who locked himself inside a downtown deli's bathroom and refused to leave. How long could he hold out? Sure, the bathroom barricade offered sufficient running water, but needed sustenance – a kitchen full of deli sandwiches – was agonizingly out of reach on the other side of an impenetrable wall. The untenability of the situation must worn down his will, for he eventually relinquished his pissoir stronghold.

**2:32 a.m.** Two Humboldt State University scholars were found wandering in circles on the southern terminus of Janes Road, bellowing about being "on their way to Arcata."

**3:23 a.m.** The passed-out drunk didn't do much to improve the glamour quotient of the cement barrier on the Seventh Street overpass.

**11:48 a.m.** Rottweiler versus a black lab? Not much of a contest, especially when the lab is leashed and the Rott is loose, running free on Trail 14 in Redwood Park. The lab wound up at the veterinarian and the more jawsome dog's owner somehow became unavailable to cover reimbursement of the $30 medical bill.

**12:55 p.m.** Fickle Hill Road residents have been seen heading home from the forest across the street with an armload of firewood, and this one was encountered by Arcata's park ranger gathering wood along Redwood Park where CDF just cleared flammable overgrowth. Caught redwood-handed, the best he could do was claim that a private tree service had given him permission to do collect the wood, which didn't win him any points with Ranger Bob. "I knew he was lying," said the patient ranger, who hasn't quite seen everything yet. The wood rustler was referred to Environmental Services.

**6:50 p.m.** A woman reported a $60 money order and an address book were stolen during a three-minute period in which her back was turned from her trailer on two different occasions. She believes that satellites have been manipulating her neighbors to sneak into her trailer and steal her belongings.

**8:11 p.m.** *Verbatim verse from the APD dispatcher log:*
Prowler on back porch
The subject turned on some kind of light
House is by the church
It is a yellow house.

**11:12 p.m.** A man reported that someone was stalking him. He knew, because he could smell a cooked animal from three miles away. The stalker hadn't contacted him and he didn't feel any danger from him, though people were trying to turn him into a woman. With that, he went to bed.

**• Saturday, March 30 2:28 a.m.** It's hard to sit up straight in the back seat of a police car for the whole eight-mile trip to the Pink House when your hands are cuffed behind you and you're drunk. Just an observation.

**10:45 a.m.** A traveler was cruelly deprived of the basic necessities for enjoying a bright spring day – his marijuana and syringe. That and the warrant landed him in the Pink House.

**3:13 p.m.** A very agitated man showed up at the station claiming a woman was going to have a baby in his car. Trouble was, he didn't know where the car was.

**3:52 p.m.** He called 911 a while later, going on about the woman being in labor. He was admonished for misusing the emergency line.

**8:57 p.m.** Arcata and HSU police converged on person reported sleeping on the 14th Street side of Redwood Park. But it was just a pile of blankets doing a Pete imitation.

**• Sunday, March 31 10:10 a.m.** The tender equipoise of a Sunday morning, balanced delicately between dewy daybreak and sparkling midday – time to hasten the weekend through by blasting everyone on I Street with one's personal music choices. Or maybe not.

**1:14 p.m.**
Out on the tracks, the Fun Bunch
Whose forties and nugs pack a punch
Police met goodtimers
Reverse social climbers
Suspected of smoking their lunch.

**8:26 p.m.** A dinner party on South G went even further south when a guest and his host had a disagreement. The guest left, then came back and broke a window, which cast something of a pall over what might have been a happy occasion.

**• April Fool's Day 1:55 p.m.** Four travelers sought succor and a buzz in a J Street alley, but those darn old bicycle cops are like stash-sucking mosquitoes, buzzing around everywhere.

• **Friday, April 5 8:29 a.m.** A classic Arcata morning loon (whose plumage included the requisite grimy knapsack) was perched out front of an I Street cooperative supermarket hooting, hollering and, *sin of sins,* hampering enjoyment of lattes and scones. Located at the Ninth and H aviary (where else?), he was taken into custody and caged on charges of possession of a concealed weapon (a knife) and probation violation.

**8:37 a.m.** Adhesive researchers may wish to study the undesired presence who managed an uncanny imitation of a barnacle at a downtown coffee temple. Police pried him loose.

**11:42 a.m.** Proving again that men will be men and find something to argue about no matter what, two fellows got yelly in an I Street parking lot over the way a dog was tied up in the bed of a truck.

**2:19 p.m.** Over-the-counter antihistamines contain an ingredient – ephedrine – which is key in methamphetamine production. Maybe the Sudafed shoplifter at an F Street supermarket wanted it for that; maybe he just had *real bad allergies.* In any case, he somehow made it out of the parking lot in a state-of-the-art crankmobile – a neon-blue Kia Sephia with broken passenger window and mirror.

**3:08 p.m.** A man called a woman at her downtown workplace two times, saying that he had been wandering the building in which she works and watching her for the last two hours. He skin-crawlingly described what she looks like and what she was wearing, too.

**10:06 p.m.** If Arcata was redesigned from scratch, the sports bar probably wouldn't share a common wall with a hotel, especially on Saturday nights.

**11:27 p.m.** Out Valley West way, a young person's Saturday Night Sociable isn't complete without the guzzling of affordable liquor, processing and excretion of same onto cars in an apartment complex parking lot.

• **Sunday, April 7 12:12 a.m.** He could probably have drawn an equally convincing an ID with thrift shop Crayolas, and probably, he should have. Citations were handed out for false identification and being a minor in a tavern.

**12:41 a.m.** With pseudonyms like Shakespeare, Shakey and Shaky – all based on an inherently wobbly phoneme – it stands to reason that the owner of the moniker was arrested on a public drunkenness charge, probation violation plus three outstanding warrants.

**1:56 a.m.** A medical cannabis clinic and auto repair shop – two separate businesses, mind you – were burgled in the 600 block of I Street.

**3:56 a.m.** What better time for a rendezvous in an Alliance Road convenience mart parking lot? And what better pursuit than practicing one's swearing skills at top volume? An officer met the consonant dispensers, sending them on their way.

**7:30 a.m.** Someone rolled a little white car down Park Avenue, positioning it against a fence as a practical joke. Once everyone recovered from the sidesplitting hilarity, wiped the tears of joy from their eyes and regained control of their respiratory functions, the little white car was moved back up the street.

**4:25 p.m.** A traveler positioned himself in front of an F Street pet shop and told passersby he was going to eat his dog. At the request of the business, the doggie diner was asked to move along.

**6:25 p.m.** Maybe her porch light had been shining into his apartment, but that's no reason to talk to her that way.

**• Monday, April 8 6:14-6:51 a.m.** He'd been drinking all night, and seemed obsessed with getting into a neighbor's apartment. There was talk of suicide and burning the neighbor's possessions. The warnings didn't take, the crazy talk continued and Big Pink absorbed yet another wayward soul.

**• Tuesday, April 9 3:47 a.m.** A Foster Avenue resident was awakened by a long-haired, drunken, disheveled traveler leaning against and banging on his back door. Rather than reach out to a fellow human and attempt to understand his special needs, the resident called police, who booked the hairy, drunken, disheveled, leaning doorbanger in the Pink House.

**8:18 a.m.** Those blue-painted, extra-wide parking spaces with a wheelchair symbol are real handy-dandy for parking your trailer in.

**5:02 p.m.** A guitarist rocked out on I Street so loudly the he couldn't even hear the neighbs banging on his door. Police penetrated the fuzztone fog and advised him to play at sub-seismic levels in the future.

**6:20 p.m.** The guitar man got mad at a neighbor he thought had called the cops, but who hadn't.

**9:32 p.m.** Guitaristics flared again on I Street, but even as the complaint was being phoned in, the volume was dialed back.

**10:42 p.m.** That white van in the 500 block of H Street must be set on a hair trigger, as its alarm is always shouting to "STAY AWAY FROM THE CAR." All the neighbors want is for the car's desultory-stentorian emanations to stay away from their ears.

**• Wednesday, April 10 10:15 a.m.**
The Fun Bunchers' daily soiree
Metastasized in its own way
Its participants
Wrecked the sweet ambiance
Of the storage space yard 'cross the way.

**• Thursday, April 11 9:04 a.m.**
Fun Bunchers' expressive caprices
Got one guy hauled off by polices
Graffiti aggression
Was soon to be freshened
Cleaned up by remaining artistes.

**2:11 p.m.**
On tracks where once cargo was freighted
A Fun Buncher, investigated
His protests deemed baseless
Was fitted with bracelets
And busted for something unstated.

**2:34 p.m.** Mom caught sonny boy charging porn on the Web with her plastic. *Oops.*

**8:13 p.m.**
Bayside Road, a deer
Speeding car in the darkness
The car's still with us.

**• Friday, April 12 1:02 a.m.**
There he was
Layin' on the street
Got the funniest looks from
Coppers on the beat
Hey hey, he's a drunky
Shoulda stopped before that last round
But he was too busy drinkin'
They put him away downtown.

**1:14 a.m.** A he and she in a car enjoyed a "loud animated discussion" which was misinterpreted – or was it? – as an argument by a concerned citizen.

**7:20 a.m.** Large plastic price sign numbers were stolen from an Alliance Road gas station. Two 3's, one 2, one zero and three 9/10's now adorn the lair of a digit ripper, as does the warm glow of accomplishment.

**12:29 p.m.** A man was assaulted from behind in what was described as an unprovoked attack at Ninth and H streets. A struggle ensued, falling far short of cinematic depictions of manly conflict, which generally involve heroic posturing, elegant choreography, well-aimed blows and a clear victor and vanquished. In reality, there was a lot of inconclusive grappling, grasping at clothing with heads down, garbled curses and swift encirclement by blue uniforms. A suspect was jailed, no one got the girl and civilization continues to be doomed by powerful evildoers.

**2:44 p.m.** Ah, a shiny new children's playground at the Community Center. *Release the hounds!*

**5:27 p.m.** Millabout alert at a Plaza liquor store.

**6:27 p.m.** Like a moth to flame, a cocktail-medicated soul staggered toward the blinding fluorescent lights of an F Street variety store, but once inside, became confused about what to do next. Police solved that conundrum, hauling him off to jail on public drunkenness and probation violation charges.

**10:54 p.m.** Party time and noise annoyance time ramped up all over town, from West End Road to 18th Street. It would be interesting to know whether, on the cosmic scale of things, the quantum amount of pleasure derived from gleeful abandon balances out the cumulative annoyance of neighbors.

• **Saturday, April 13 7:44 a.m.** More gas price numbers disappeared overnight. What some special someone is going to do with two more big plastic "9/10" signs is not known.

**8 a.m.** A Wilson Street resident said that several days earlier, a woman identifying herself only as a member of "the coalition" had asked about the well-being of a neighbor's dog. Later, the woman was seen entering a backyard and heading towards a dog pen. Reported as a possible theft, the incident was documented.

**1:08 p.m.** A customer who arrived at a Seventh Street bank just after closing time was unable to transact business, and did the only logical thing – began punching at the windows.

• **Sunday, April 14 11:48 a.m.**
On F Street, somebody was grumbling
Of laundromat lingerers bumbling
And hanging about
They said they'd get out
As soon as their clothes were done tumbling.

**4:10 p.m.** Some people with a pickup truck full of frozen meat of questionable origin were trying to sell same door to door. On the subject of business licenses, the roving animal part vendors were vague. They got as far as Devlin Court before police were called.

• **Tuesday, April 16 2:01 p.m.** The cosmic statistical imperative dictates that there must be one lingering freak in every Arcata parking lot who just can't get it through his head that he isn't wanted there.

**3:19 p.m.** If what police say is true, a young man attempted to take something from an I street cooperative supermarket that didn't even belong to him. It gets worse. Evidently the lad has taken a very wrong turn and begun experimenting with marijuana. Right here. In our town.

• **Wednesday, April 17 1:19 a.m.**
A Valley East tune-lovin' dude
Did not moderate amplitude
The neighbors, awakened
From walls that were shakin'
Called cops, who restored quietude.

**1:45 p.m.** A little opossum family – a mama and her two babies – came to a bad end in the roadway, 1600 block of H Street. Too badly injured to survive, the critters were taken to the Corp Yard and humanely put down.

**2:38 p.m.** Don't give money to voices on the phone. Or do, and wind up getting written about here.

**4:58 p.m.** Real campers pitch their tent in the Trinity Alps, not Trail 1 in the Arcata Community Forest.

**5:42 p.m.** Also on Trail 1, just up the way, a man was cited for two dog violations and a pair of outstanding warrants.

**5:48 p.m.** At an F Street supermarket, someone grabbed "a bottle" – probably not celery juice – and ran out without paying for it, but not before being recognized by the guard.

• **Thursday, April 18 12:37 a.m.** An aggressive Rottweiler chased cars at Alliance Road and Spear Avenue.

**6:03 p.m.** Roommate relations dipped a tad when a woman reported a surveillance camera having been placed in her room.

• **Saturday, April 20 1:10 a.m.** Two parties kludged together near Alliance Road and Spear Avenue. Tons of cars, noise, the whole bit.

**1:26 a.m.** Sophisticates on upper H Street gathered for highbrow hijinks distinguished by blasting music, yelling, banging things and even jumping up and down. The hostess agreed to quell the genteel social pursuits.

**1:57 a.m.** In the 2900 block of Mack Road, party-time jollity included loud people and music, plus "strange flashes."

**2:12 a.m.** An allegedly drunken traveler staggered into a perpetual donut mecca, where he was arrested on multiple warrants and a public drunkenness charge, then Pink Housed.

**4:57 a.m.** Every morning, neighbors say, the dog in Tina Court wakes up about this time, and so must they.

**11:28 a.m.** Fun Bunchers celebrated the Holiest of Holy holidays, attracting police to what must be the most well-furnished train tracks in the universe.

**4:34 p.m.** All kinds of cars were parked in the area of Park Avenue and Fickle Hill Road as their drivers went to smoke dope in Redwood Park. This year, APD's presence at 420 was minimal and limited to calls for service, but none were received.

• **Sunday, April 21 1:59 a.m.** Bar closing time, and fists bloomed like five-fingered flowers just south of an historic Plaza storehouse.

**11:13 a.m.**
'Twixt train track and overgrown bramble
Fun Bunchers cavort and like, gambol
Some jesting, some joking
Perhaps sometimes toking
Till p'licemen swing through on a ramble.

**1:11 p.m.** The question is, who hangs on to his all-weather guitar when the Fun Bunch's premier bluesman spends a stint in the Pink House on a public drunkenness charge?

**1:51 p.m.** With guitarless bluesman in custody, an officer backed his cruiser into the fence by the mammoth compost heap, causing minor damage.

**Guitar Dan entertains the Breakfast Club/Fun Bunch.**

• **Monday, April 22 1:13 a.m.** What the – ?

**3:36 a.m.** Not again!

**6:14 a.m.** Too much.

**6:28 a.m.** Why?

**3:11 p.m.** A cocktail-enraptured man settled down for a siesta on the sidewalk in the 1500 block of G Street.

**10:49 p.m.** A woman left the hospital before she could be detained by staff, who said she had taken some 20 to 25 15 milligram Welbutrin tablets, had been drinking and who had methamphetamine "on board." She was located and returned to the hospital.

• **Tuesday, April 23 12:15 a.m.** A person passing through the 1100 block of K Street came upon a shopping cart in the roadway. When he went to move the obstruction, a bearded figure approached in a state of defensive aggression, as though the citizen were a competing Neanderthal attempting to steal a fresh heap of carrion. Grasped in the bearded one's hand was that timeless symbol of humanity – a fist-clenched stick, with which the passerby was warded away from the marooned cart. Police were called, arrived and were "out with cart," but the bearded one, his stick, pea coat and baseball cap were nowhere to be found.

**1:33 a.m.** They told her she was in no condition to leave the ER. "You're in no condition to leave the ER," they said. So what did she do? Leave the ER. Police found her at a strip mall across the freeway. She struggled a bit until they strapped her into the bed, then wisely surrendered to the inevitable.

**2:44 p.m.** A redwood forest as cherished as the one off 14th Street should never have drug-addled bozos wandering its trails.

**2:58 p.m.** An F Street handicapped parking spot reserved for those who need as much close access as possible should never be occupied by a lazy non-disabled person.

**5 p.m.** Same handicapped parking spot as before; same $330 fine for a different lazy-abled person.

• **Wednesday, April 24 5:21 a.m.** Her version: He tried to assault her and busted up her stuff, then took off. His version: He accidentally broke a lamp and cut himself before departure.

**1:01 p.m.** In the greenest part of the lower forest, just up the trail from the 14th Street gate, a he and she allegedly broke out their own green – nugs. Things got greener still, when a uniformed park ranger appeared unexpectedly. His ticket book was soon two lighter.

**2:21 p.m.** A high school student said he was bitten by a "pocket gopher" at school.

**4:55 p.m.** A person reported threats by a housemate. The accused said the accuser was harassing him. As you can see, the rough parity of their competing claims created something of a moral stalemate.

**9:11 p.m.** A car crashed into a building in the 400 block of G Street, then did something the building couldn't do – drove off northbound on G Street.

**11:35 p.m.** A big whoop-te-do wingding in a budget motel room in Valley West didn't shut down without some hard feelings.

• **Thursday, April 25 1:26 a.m.** Ongoing field research by those wanted on warrants as to how to best attract police attention bore fruit once again. A vehicle at Tenth and I streets had a license plate which didn't match, and it wasn't long before an officer found out about that messy business back east. Shortly, the suspect found himself stewing in the Pink House with a lot to look forward to – extradition to Logan, Utah.

**11:22 a.m.** A fare obstinately refused to pay the cab driver, and instead took a seat out front of a Plaza tavern/taxidermy museum. There, he was cited for the cab fare holdout, which, incongruously, qualifies as "defrauding an innkeeper."

**12:02 p.m.** A casually attired man appeared at a Villa Way home wielding a dirty spray bottle and offering to sell some sort of dubious cleaning supplies. When the front door was closed on him, he left, but not before taking a lingering look at the resident's property. The grunge salesman and his baggy shorts were intercepted a ways away, and told all about things that big grown-up door-to-door solicitors should have, like business permits. The man turned out to be with the very reputable-sounding Hy-Pro Cleaners, a Texas firm whose local branch was operating out of Room 132 in a Eureka motel.

**4:17 p.m.** Her neighbor keeps dinging her car door with his car door, she claims. Plus he's being a dick about it.

**6:07 p.m.** A Northtown mini-mart's bathroom was mercilessly monkey-wrenched by a person for whom counseling might be a serious consideration. Whoever it was broke the toilet handle off and tossed it into the toilet itself, then made a "large mess" with available materials and selected personal emissions. Police investigation confirmed the broken handle, but could not determine intentional mischief to the fixture. What was certain was that someone had taken the trouble to pee in the scrub brush holder – like the flush handle caper, a reversible situation given proper attention by a designated wage slave. The sundered water closet was rehabilitated and the entire urine-drenched imbroglio documented.

**6:29 p.m.** More faucet crises, this time on Old Arcata Road where a "gravely injured" deer was cowering under a plumbing fixture. Approached, Bambi bounded off looking A-OK.

**9:21 p.m.** A Plaza import shop has inherited the nightly retinue of alcohol-fueled sidewalk warmers who seek succor in its recessed doorway, which is what led the shoe shop to flee the Plaza. This night, police waded into the nest of scrounge lizards, seized a bottle of something. Soon the gutter burbled merrily with free-flowing spirits, liquid variety.

• **Sunday, April 26 12:49 a.m.** More nocturnal auto maintenance – this time with the bonus yelling feature – on Susan Street. Kids at the green house agreed to quieten down.

**12:53 a.m.** Further balcony antics, with yelling – screaming too, according to the dispatcher log – plus loud, loud music. Everyone inside.

**7:26 a.m.** A deluxe eviction on L.K. Wood included a restraining order to get the tenant out and keep him away for good.

**9:14 a.m.**
A rhododendron
They dug at, but couldn't steal
Like, how lame is that?

**12:45 p.m.** A black lab left in a car at 15th and F had no food or water, both of which are real handy for sustaining mammalian life functions. Police left a note.

**1:06 p.m.** *This just in* – you aren't supposed to chug weed while you're on probation.

**4:29 p.m.** More drama than usual at a Northtown burrito palace.

**8:32 p.m.** A South H Street woman looked out her front window and observed an unusual addition to the neighborhood – a man puking his guts out on the sidewalk. He was next seen trying to get inside a white truck. Police arrested him on a public drunkenness charge, and transported him, sans stomach contents, to the Pink House.

**10:28 p.m.** A J street woman nipped out to the store for a few minutes, and came back to find her home splat-slathered with paintballs.

• **Monday, April 27 12:18 a.m.** Beguzzled gladiators clashed outside a Plaza tavern. In a clinch, the two fell to earth, where they struggled for ascendancy on the spittle-pocked pavement, then lost interest and ran off before police arrived.

**12:56 a.m.** Does it ever cross the minds of people making hella noise late at night like the ones on Acheson Way that their shouting might be kind of obnoxious for neighbors? The Golden Rule's beacon of fair play having failed to penetrate the dark night of selfishness, a more potent noise citation was deployed to helpful effect.

**One time a bunch of person-sized metal pods with hinged entry hatches appeared around town. It turned out a sculptor had moved away and left the enigmatic items behind.**

**1:31 a.m.** The perfect end to a perfect night at a Chester Avenue party – a front lawn fight involving eight to 10 menfolk. They scattered.

**10:14 a.m.** To some, noisy car maintenance is like astronomy – best performed at night. Police will be patrolling the 1400 block of S Street, listening for cargazers.

**7:23 p.m.** Minstrels through the ages have been hounded and squelched as they refined their craft, and the band in Todd Court kept up the tradition.

**8:38 p.m.** Todd Court's bass player got in a few more licks, and a warning notice was issued.

**• Tuesday, April 28 6:35 a.m.** Someone threw an orange juice container in the middle of a Valley West parking lot.

**5:01 p.m.** A visiting San Franciscan let his three-legged dog run loose in Valley West, and it unevenly chased a kid into the street. The owner was advised of leash laws, and apologized.

**• Wednesday, April 29 12:03 a.m.** A 19-year-old tried to get an over-21 person to buy alcohol for him at an F Street supermarket, and got into a dispute with store personnel when they refused to sell it. The booze-seeking missile and a colleague had launched to parts unknown when police arrived...

**12:44 a.m.** ... but came back with their special needs, and weren't wanted. Again they bolted before police arrived...

**5:01 p.m.** ...and a few minutes later police chatted with two nightcrawlers at a Fourth Street store.

**12:57 p.m.** APD helped HSU PD with two dogs tied up and lunging at passersby at the parking meters by the gym. The owner carred the toothsome twosome.

• **Friday, May 3 12:54 a.m.** "Get off me!" yelled the woman in the house near the gas station, so loud it was heard by neighbors. Protective forces descended, found another knotty he-she dispute and passed out marital aids – social service referral cards.

**2:47 a.m.** They may not have thought anyone would see them hop the fence into her yard, but a resident did, and called police. Police were there in a flash. Two were detained on scene, but the one dressed in black ran down the train tracks a ways before being caught. Chances are the public drunkenness, pot possesh and prowling charges won't show up on their resumés, unless there's a hiring fair at Sneaky Nitwit Corp.

**12:22 p.m.** A woman felt like that guy on the bus was stalking her. He said that he doesn't relate well to women. That's as may be, explained an officer, but you oughtn't follow her; just leave her alone. He accepted the assignment.

**12:39 p.m.** A cataclysmic clash of wills took place in the drive-thru lane at a Valley West burger stand, with one point of view articulated by a sub-orbital soda. Police found the beverage launcher cowering behind the pizza parlor. Burger officials reported that he'd thrown the soda at her, but she wasn't talking. She conceded only that the soda – flavor unspecified – had been flung, but not at what or whom. It wasn't the best use of 14 minutes and 24 seconds of police time.

**12:48 p.m.** If only people could know they were going to stay together or not before they procreate.

**2:32 p.m.** That's it – she's getting Caller ID on her phone.

**5:02 p.m.** The more percussive phonemes in someone's 800-word vocabulary were hastily cobbled together to insult an answering machine, which dutifully recorded the verbal abuse, then beeped in chipper acknowledgment.

**5:11 p.m.** Wow, a downtown parking place! Right next to this row of blue metal boxes with slots.

**8:03 p.m.** A she-ex complained that he-ex was late – an *hour* late – returning their embattled spawn from a visitation. When he-ex did show up, his car was belching smoke, and that seemed to corroborate his excuse.

**8:39 p.m.** A semi-impromptu concert took place in front of a G Street movie theatre which is painfully transmogrifying into a concert hall. Unable to take the uncertified stage inside, a band *just happened* to show up with a generator to power a streetside performance, which is either like totally cool or completely inappropriate.

**• Saturday, May 4 12:54 a.m.** A man loaned his car keys to a friend – always a wise move – who said she wouldn't return them. She, resplendent in green Army jacket and lip ring, had left a hour ago. Next, a search of the bars.

**3:59 a.m.** Maybe in his allegedly cocktail-besotted mind, pounding on a woman's door and refusing to leave made perfect sense. He had a lot of time to reconsider in the Pink House.

**5:19 a.m.** When a man showed up "out of the blue" at a West End Road business offering four knives for sale, it seemed a little strange. Now, the next day, it seemed a little worrisome, in case the guy might come back and do something criminal. Police checked around the place, and all seemed normal.

**8:43 a.m.** A man called 911 at 8:43 a.m. because he was out of beer, and that's an emergency.

**9:02 a.m. – 12:08 p.m.** Police devoted shoe leather to occasional hot spots, including the train tracks by the storage yard, the I Street boat basin, the Plaza, a Uniontown shopping center, Redwood Park and upper elevations thereof.

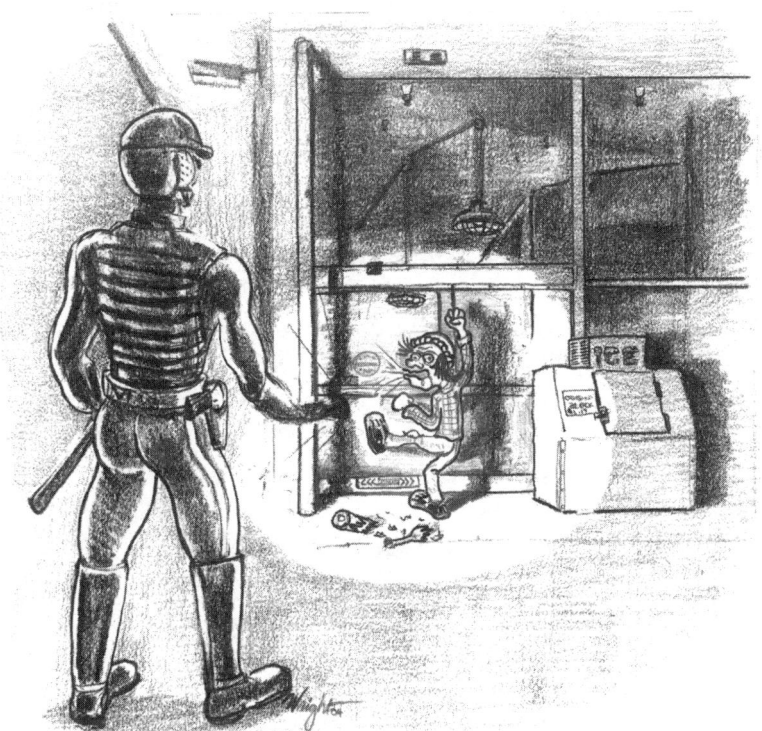

**11:42 p.m.** Another re-enactment of *The Days of Wine and Roses* as an unsatisfied tippler pounded futilely on the door of a 13th Street marketplace, only to be scraped away and drunk tanked.

**11:52 p.m.**
A lost dog in a Plaza hotel
Wandered halls, trapped in right-angle hell
Didn't know what to do
And it snarled some, too
But when master appeared, all was well.

• **Sunday, May 5 12:44 a.m.** If the measure of a party's success is the density of the broken bottles and cars parked on neighbor's lawns – and it is – then the bash on Old Arcata Road was as good as it gets.

**12:43– 2:31 a.m.** Not to be outdone, parties on Redwood Avenue, Valley West Boulevard, 18th Street and Granite Avenue took up police time.

**11 a.m.**
At Ninth and H streets, a loose dog
Was trotting around on a jog
Its clue-challenged friend
Got a ticket just then
Which perhaps penetrated his fog.

**12:19 p.m.** The population of Fun Bunch World Headquarters out by the tracks was reduced by one when a traveler was arrested on marijuana and probation violation charges. He was also accused of packing some kind of modern substance which only a pharmaceutical manufacturer, wholesaler, pharmacy, physician, podiatrist, dentist, veterinarian, certified nurse-midwife, nurse practitioner or physician assistant is supposed to have – and even then only when in stock containers correctly labeled with the name and address of the supplier or producer. Apparently, very few of the above hang out on the tracks with the Bunch.

**3:08 p.m.** When the Creator designed opossums, she somehow misread the instructions. The part that said "add brains" she took to say "beat with ugly stick." That may explain the expired unit in the 1300 block of K Street, which likely stared snaggle-toothed and dumbfounded at a hurtling vehicle till the very end.

**6:45 p.m.** A woman complained that her ex was 25 minutes late for a child custody exchange, then refused to take the child's prescription medicine with him (his girlfriend did grab it) and didn't even have a legally required car seat.

**8:41 p.m.** On Hallen Drive, a suspect/performance artist allegedly broke a sliding glass door, punched holes in three closets, then hung around to be arrested on three warrants and jailed.

**9:44 p.m.** That was some creative parking, the way that truck stuck out diagonally on Park Avenue. The tow truck driver probably stowed it in a more conventional fashion back at the storage yard.

**• Monday, May 6 8:07 a.m.** Someone thought a trav was sleeping under the City Hall flagpole, but it was just a pile of trash, soon incarcerated in a dumpster.

**8:13 a.m.** Two travelers who had been trying to peddle some hand tools up and down Ninth Street were cordially bad vibed.

**11:38 a.m.** Marijuana addicts dosed up in the nether region along the north side of the Intermodal Transient Facility.

**1:51 p.m.** The Hallen Drive closet puncturer was back at it, and had allegedly diversified his talent portfolio to include ripping a screen door off its hinges and breaking a lamp along with adding an additional hole to the closet. A judge declined to issue an emergency protective order, and recommended instead that a domestic violence restraining order be sought through the courts.

**2:44 p.m.** A traveler was arrested on a petty theft charge at an I Street cooperative supermarket. How original.

**4:16 p.m.** A Trinidad resident was cited for petty theft at an I Street cooperative supermarket. Ditto.

**• Tuesday, May 7 6:19 p.m.** If I only had a brain. *(Obscene and annoying phone calls on B Street.)*

**6:30 p.m.** A heart. *(A violent-behaving man driving off from upper H Street with a beer in his hand.)*

**7:19 p.m.** A home. *(An unruly herd of travelers scattering garbage, skating and making a ruckus in an H Street alley.)*

• **Wednesday, May 8 8:32 a.m.** *Note to self:* For better service, refrain from throwing punches at the receptionist.

**10:38 a.m.** Acting on the theory that there isn't enough insensate howling in the world, a man took it upon himself to rectify matters. He was warned about trespassing.

**12:20 p.m.** Stoned and stinko at the bus station. Had Janis survived, there might be a song about this.

**2:07 p.m.** He's only out from behind bars on the condition that he stay out of places where alcohol is the main commodity. But there he was, seen skulking into a Plaza liquor store. *Oops.*

**10:03–10:44 p.m.** Sex offenders checked in with police as required by an unsmiling judge.

• **Thursday, May 9 3:19 a.m.** If not now, when? If not him, who? If not here, where? The 100 block of Samoa Boulevard, where a bout of solo utility pole-gripping was the pastime du noir. A witness observing the man's liberties with the utility stanchion called police, who arrived after the fellow had satisfied himself (and hopefully, pleasured the pole, too) and moved along.

**11:20 a.m.** The fair maiden's kisses were like sweet, sweet wine, except that the maiden was actually a 24-oz. can of low-buck, high-kick hooch which wasn't wine, it was that bastard child of the brewer's art, a carbonated malt beverage providing the morning's effervescence. Alas, for a boy-child in Redwood Park's 14th Street lot, this is a forbidden love, whose ambrosial moment yielded to coarser textures – cop car vinyl and clammy steel bars.

**2:01 p.m.** A Parks Department employee hailed an officer after someone on the Plaza threw a loaf of bread at him.

**2:35 p.m.** Freeway tensions followed some people to Redwood Park, where they yelled at each other ineffectually amid the soaring redwoods.

**3:44 p.m.** An I Street man's guitar playing inspired a neighbor to singing. Well, actually yelling. At him. About the playing.

**7:36 p.m.** And now for something completely different – *yelling!* It was a woman's nephew, using the phone for conveyance of top-volume obscenities.

• **Friday, May 10 11:29 a.m.** The office of a Valley West burger franchise is no sanctuary from purse thieves.

**12:10 p.m.** An elderly green Oldsmobile lumbered into the intersection of Alliance Road and Foster Avenue, died, then started up again. Like the old, tired company that manufactured it, the hunk of Detroit iron clung to life a little longer before succumbing to reality.

**1:47 p.m.** Two men were reportedly found in Redwood Park possessing a leafy substance which, when smoked, induces "happy anxiety" marked by lightheaded giddiness, altered perception and the eventual onset of "the munchies," during which things like pistachios, root beer, pizza, stale Triscuits and, oh hell, basically anything in the fridge tastes like provender of the gods. Or so we've heard.

**2:45 p.m.** Hello. A big snake came through the ceiling and dropped down into a Valley West store. It was returned to the nearby pet shop.

**11:42 p.m.** Harsh words in front of a Valley West burger franchise. The alleged argument migrated to a nearby gas station, where police found the group enmeshed in a controversy over how to get to the Mad River.

**11:49 p.m.** An unknown substance had been spread over the pay telephone in front of an F Street supermarket, and when the heavy-set man with a goatee used the phone, some of the ick got in his ear. This really set him off, and he was described as irate, angry and creating a disturbance. The goo victim and his polluted ear were asked to leave and not come back. The substance was not identified, and that's just as well.

• **Saturday, May 11 1:03 a.m.** A Plaza tavern asked that a sidewalk drummer stop tormenting a bongo, and, incidentally, everyone else within earshot.

**2:25 a.m.** Representatives of the hairier, scarier, more frequently unruly gender became overly animated outside an H Street deli.

**2:24 p.m.** He thought he was in the legendary Emerald City of Arcata, where the City Council is Green, the forests are greener and that with which one stokes one's bowl is the greenest yet. Ah, but that one-time reality has given way to a new paradigm, where granola is inevitably laced with GMOs, panhandlers drive SUVs, Lassie must be leashed and City cops also wear green and are called park rangers. Thus, the habitue of the former druggie meadow in Redwood Park was brought up to date in the current events curve when he met a kindly ranger and bade regretful farewell his stash.

**2:36 p.m.** At the request of a citizen, oblivious Redwood Park picnickers were asked to turn their boom boxes down to a somewhat less thunderous level.

**8:11 p.m.** The Story of Man, excerpted verbatim from the

official dispatcher bulletin:
...Crashing and female crying
Children in house
Has heard babies
White car driving away...
Male was gone on arrival.

**9:10 p.m.** A confused calf got loose on Q Street, and likely experienced the bovine equivalent of relief when it was repasture-ized.

• **Saturday, May 12 12:29 a.m.** While a victim received emergency treatment at the hospital, a slithery subhuman life form bashed in the victim's car window and stole a wallet.

• **Monday, May 13 7:05 a.m.** The tradition of Arcata flag stealing was revived when City Hall's banners vanished. Though a 1995 flag theft was followed by an anonymous Anti-Nixon diatribe, opposition to Tricky appears to have been superseded by more contemporary concerns, as no follow-up statement was received.

**11:30 a.m.** Four teenagers took a bottle of Southern Comfort from a Valley West food place, ferried it to a safe remove and tried not to visibly shudder in front of each other as each swig of the vile potion assaulted their olfactory apparati.

• **Tuesday, May 14 2:18 a.m.** You missed out on the scintillating repartee and spitting at the very exclusive soiree behind the H Street donut shop this particular a.m. Police harshed away the nightcrawlers.

**3:32 p.m.** A McKinleyviller made a memorable impression for her creative driving. The car was found in front of a Plaza tavern, but she didn't seem drunk. She explained that she had trouble making the vehicle veer properly and the wind makes this problem even worse.

**6:37 p.m.** A traveler visiting Redwood Park enjoyed so much liquid refreshment that he was to be hauled away by police.

**9:32 p.m.** Battling skateboarders made their way through Northtown, taking turns bopping each other with their boards. At some point they separated and police couldn't find them.

**• Wednesday, May 15 7:37 a.m.** If you wanted to just nosh your bagel and sip your coffee in peace, that privilege was denied you by the mouthy wingnut on I Street.

**12:06 p.m.**
Fun Bunchers, those lovable lugs
Were found with the tracks where they chugs
Their bowl-horns o' plenty
Two pot-cognoscente
Were cited and stripped of their nugs.

**1:59 p.m.** It was 3 a.m. when an Alliance Road resident was called an unspecified naughty name. The name-caller then pledged to have the puzzled woman arrested, but didn't say for what. The rest of the night passed uneventfully, but around 6: 30 or 7 a.m., she heard someone making phony crow sounds from the other side of a fence. Just when things couldn't get any weirder, a megaphone-amplified voice from a nearby gas station boomed, "WHAT ARE YOU DOING THERE?" It was the second night in a row this had happened.

**• Thursday, May 16 8:09 p.m.** A group of people had gathered in front of the yellow house, and a cursory vibescan of emanations issuing therefrom indicated to a neighbor that either a fight was brewing after an argument, or an argument was brewing after a fight. Actually, it was a barbecue.

**• Friday, May 17 7:33 a.m.** A guy on the lam from Crescent City wound up snared in the lines of flux emanating from

Arcata's own freak magnet, the Redwood Park 14th Street lot. He was disentangled, arrested and deposited in the Pink House.

**12:43 p.m.** An officer held frank, temporarily productive discussions with the Fun Bunch, the benefit of which dissipated like wisps of bong exhaust in the wind as soon as the cop took his leave.

**2:49 p.m.** On any given day, she said, 20 or so callers pay a very brief visit to her neighbor's home. But twice a month – on payday – the number of short-term visitors zooms to 50 or 60 per day, each roaring up, sprinting inside with the motor left running and then hurriedly departing mere moments later. That's hardly enough time for a decent hand of bridge, a diverting taffy pull or a meaningful throw of the Tarot. Could it be... *drugs?*

**3:52 p.m.** Personnel at an I Street cooperative supermarket so look forward to the day when they never see this pain-in-the-entrance guy again.

**4:22 p.m.** Two travelers in Redwood Park set to sea in a bowl... But it wasn't the sea, it was the big green water tank they huddled near. And the bowl was at the end of a groovy glass pipe. Well, when Ranger Bob happened by, just imagine the wacky hijinx that ensued.

**10:03 p.m.**
A young bongoist took up station
In front of a tavern location
His joyful hand drumming
Had customers bumming
Annoyed by the lad's inspiration.

• **Saturday, May 18 12:35 a.m.** It wasn't that this guy's

pants were baggy, but they were, or that his ball cap bespoke yokelhood, although it did... No, the problem was behavioral – his halitosis-based belligerence and the near-certainty that he would irrevocably harsh the free-flowing camaraderie found at this friendly Plaza tavern. With assistance from police, the host organism expelled the foreign matter.

**1:47 a.m.** A couple awoke, tried to work out some personal problems, then went back to sleep.

**8 a.m.** A man selling flowers out of a van assured police that yes, he did have a business license, *yep, sure, uh-huh,* got one of those all right. *What?* Oh, well, not *with* me. The officer suggested that further research would be helpful.

• **Sunday, May 19 12:10 a.m.** Someone got drunk in a bar.

**1:47 a.m.** Someone got drunk and got in a fight in front of a bar.

**1:53 a.m.** Someone got in a fight across the Plaza from the bars.

**2:07 a.m.** Someone got drunk on the Plaza.

**2:15 a.m.** Someone else got drunk on the Plaza.

**The 700 block of Ninth Street – Tavern Row.**

# TERRENCE MCNALLY'S
# TAVERN
# ROW TALES

**H**eading downtown of a Friday Night, the neon lit martini glass signs of Arcata's Tavern Row beckon – a gin-soaked oasis. Step over the sprawled bodies of Plazoids while ignoring their "Spare a nug?" entreaty. Hop the butt-littered gutters and duck the clouds of smoke blowing from kicked-out college kids.

Outside it might be midnight, but walking into any of the bars along Tavern Row and they'd look much as they did a century ago. The central figure, the room-length wooden bar, is where it's always been.

Covering a block along the Plaza's north side, the facilities housing four remaining bars – the Alibi, Toby & Jack's, The Sidelines and Everett's – have been pulling suds under a variety of names and through a variety of laws. While fires have come and gone, the lots, the footprints of downtown real estate, have been serving for at least 120 years.

They're all parked there because of a one-time City ordinance that situated Arcata's watering holes within easy-walking distance of the police station. And today, it's the Department of Alcoholic Beverage Control's main concern about A-Town's taverns – too many inebriated folks stuffed into a relatively small geographical space.

Closing – bar time 2 a.m. – the bouncers clear the rooms, the imbibed spill out onto the sidewalks to follow up on long, meaningful looks under low lighting.

## Those natty gents of old...

Or to catch up on old beefs.

They hook up. They fight. The cops come. "It's a real mess of people," says Steve DeMarino, who did seven years of bouncing for Toby & Jack's bar. He's heard all the worst pickup lines over the years. "Nice shoes. Let's go to bed," still resonates as an all-time groaner. But he'd be quickly distracted from clumsy love by the boneheads debating monosyllabic showdowns before commencing in sloppy roundhouse fisticuffs. "I think it changed in 2000, or 2001," he says about outdoor Plaza behavior. "They stopped taking 'no' for an answer."

According to Dave Clark, who served up drinks at the Alibi for 17 years, nighttime Arcata wasn't always ruled by the Humboldt State University student brigade who've taken root. Arcata's bars have historically been the domain of the mainly afterwork crowd. Laborers from downtown's California Barrel Factory or the plethora of local mills made Tavern Row hum along bubbly for over a century. With multiple shifts running, quitting time was for many as early as 2 or 3 p.m. and they'd all come down for a post-shift drink. Most establishments carried pool, shuffleboard tables and dartboards. But only Toby and Jack's continues the tradition of monthly pool and dart tournaments.

But things weren't necessarily any more tame in the past, even with the competition outlets. "People would say: 'If you couldn't fight then don't come down here,'" says Clark. "The old guard of Arcata were a bunch of boozing fighters," he contends.

With one officer on duty during the day and two at night, the taverns did much of the policing themselves. Today, the Arcata Police Department is regularly circling the Plaza with three to four patrol cars on a Friday and Saturday night. According to Arcata Police Chief Randy Medosa, his department devotes 90 percent of its resources to containing the Plaza mayhem on those nights. And it's not enough.

But there were more bars then – such as The Boot, The Office, Buck's Tavern and Marino's Club. Several had three bouncers on hand to keep the peace or to stand off bemusedly for a particularly good bout. Jack Wilson recalls a tamer Tavern Row, however. Since the mid-'50s, he's owned Toby & Jack's – Arcata's stalwart redbrick drinkery. During Prohibition as the White Front (it had two stories and a dancehall upstairs), it

**...really enjoyed their Arcata taverns.**

survived on bootlegging – passing booze while the police were away. And it experienced a heyday during the 1940s, '50s and '60s when it was the place for local working folk to come together. Old timers still know it as the No Slack Saloon. The bartenders then, and arguably still, don't give no slack.

Jack started tending bar when he was 21. And yes, he admits there were some wild nights. There are still a couple bullet holes in the wall where he accidentally fired a rifle through TJ's walls. Ma Buck came into her neighboring Buck's Café the next morning to discover pots and pans dented by rounds. "Things would get pretty lively. But there wasn't the dope in those days – the marijuana and heroin people use now. If it was done, it wasn't known."

Maybe the dreads and bongos were lacking back in the day. But there weren't any fewer characters. Morris Moxon used to ride his horse through the establishments. At least once, he four-footed it up to the third floor, taking the Jacoby's Storehouse elevator up to Youngberg's.

According to Clark, as the local timber industry began to wane and HSU students began exacting more influence downtown, the clientele began to change. "In about '90 there was a real upturn in the college kids. Most of the bars started catering to them more," he says," Until about 7 or 8 p.m. the older regulars can still count on their barstool. After that the songs on the Alibi's jukebox start getting edgier, the black clothing fills the booths and the locals clear out.

"A lot of people didn't want the college trade," says Clark. He'd be the first to call himself an old timer, but Clark didn't have any qualms about serving the younger set. For one thing, Clark enjoyed most of them. "The kids treated me well. I've always prided myself on treating everybody the same. I never had to worry about closing up at two or three in the morning and have somebody waiting for me."

And working on tips, Clark pleasantly discovered

**Never a dull moment at the Logger Bar in Blue Lake, next door to Arcata.**

the Alibi's new patrons to be free with the cash. "I noticed that the college kids – they drink the expensive booze and they drink the expensive beer," The locals kept to domestic brews and cheap shots. Catering to the 20-somethings entailed stocking higher-end liquor and being prepared to mix myriad fancy concoctions. And, unlike the wage earners that had hightailed it, the kids tipped. "With the old timers, you were lucky if you made enough money in tips to buy a pack of cigarettes. And cigarettes were 50 cents back then."

That's a line repeated verbatim by Wilson at Toby and Jack's. He admits that with many of his old friends gone, working the bar at Toby and Jack's no longer has the same social relevance it once held. But the money's better.

With increased regulation, smoking kicked to the curb, ABC fines hanging over a bartender's head and a increasingly aggressive street culture, serving booze has become much more of a business than a half century ago, figures Wilson. But he shrugs, "I like people. I still do."                                                    – *T.M.*

**2:21 a.m.** It's a not-abnormal stage of development for a teenager to clamber out a bedroom window in search of wee-hour adventure, but still understandably upsetting for a parent who thinks back to when they did the same.

**2:35 a.m.** Nice party. Now, thought the hostess, where did my jewelry go?

**3:25 a.m.** A drunken clod stumbled into someone's backyard on Sixth Street, so the lord of the manor went out to confront the clod with a stick. But the hasty cudgel proved unnecessary, as police came and arrested the interloper of a public drunk charge.

**4:26 a.m.** A hit-and-run case was initiated after a man was whamsmacked at Sunset Avenue and Ross Street.

**11:35 a.m.** Someone smashed a window and spray painted a school wall on Buttermilk Lane, then consigned themselves to a still more thermally intense level of hell by littering – throwing the can in someone's yard.

**7:19 p.m.** A cat didn't qualify for a 10th life. Its remains were transported from Giuntoli Lane to the Corp Yard.

**7:20 p.m.** There were three versions of the way a traveler treated his dog in the 14th Street Redwood Park lot. The initial report held that he hung the dog by its chain leash. When police arrived, someone said he had actually swung the dog by the neck with a rope. His version was that he had merely lifted the dog by the scruff of its neck. Two travelers were warned about animal cruelty.

**• Monday, May 20 10:15 a.m.** A chap in an I Street lot tugged on an armored car's door handle as if it was a slot machine lever ready to pay off big. This got police interested in him and a colleague, and so did their outstanding warrants. Cuff-clinked and Pinked.

**3:20 p.m.** A man in a tan pickup truck pumped $17.85 in gas, then came into the Giuntoli Lane mini-mart, used the bathroom and left. But as we go to press, that's not how you pay for petrol.

**6:51 p.m.** A rude panhandler on H Street got a talking to, but the toughlove didn't take and he went right back to bothering people. He was citizen's arrested on a charge of using offensive language with the potential to provoke an immediate violent reaction.

• **Tuesday, May 21 2:53 a.m.** A purple-shirted man got shot up with demerol at the ER, then hopped in his light-colored old Ford and went for a serenely oblivious drive.

**12:11 p.m.** A godawful-gaudy orange car trolling slowly through the South I Street Marsh parking lot? Well, anyone would be suspicious.

**2:24 p.m.**
Living with you is
Doors slamming, all day, all night
And paranoia.

**3:32 p.m.** Identical twin menfolk said an employee at an Arcata business owed them money and reportedly tried to enter the business to confront the debtor, even jumping over a counter at one point. One of them allegedly said they'd be laying in wait when the employee got off work. They were gone when police arrived, and no one was exactly sure who'd made the threat, since they were, after all, twins.

**5:18 p.m.**
Four stoners were somewhat crestfallen
When Park Ranger Bob came a-callin'
He took all their doobs
And left the poor rubes
With naught to inhale but pollen.

**8:53 p.m.** A drunken, boozy-breathed man wandered around Valley West carrying a toddler and panhandling. Police escorted him to a nearby motel to make sure there was at least one sober adult around to care for the child. His wife hadn't been drinking, and both were advised to stay in the room with the little one.

• **Wednesday, May 22 9:39 a.m.** An evicted tenant left behind a filthy apartment and a dead car. Though his mom didn't agree, the landlords figured his computer and camera would just about cover the expenses.

**6:16 p.m.** It looked like a street skirmish in the battle of the sexes – groups of boys and girls confronting each other at Janes and Vaissade roads. This time, the cinematic gender tension actually turned out to be a movie in the making.

**7:09 p.m.** It wouldn't be a Saturday night without a front yard bellow or two.

• **Friday, May 24 1:30 a.m.** A landlord/tenant dispute being the perfect situation to add alcohol to, a purportedly pickled property owner reportedly claimed tenants hadn't paid up. Mounting an incursion from a driveway base of operations, he allegedly broke into the home, then changed locks.

**2:02 a.m.** He may not have been the ideal houseguest – he was "scruffy," and she'd never seen him before. And yet there he was inside her home. Fortunately, he huffed, scruffed, reversed direction and went outside, but then tried to come back in. By then the door was locked, and after some pounding, he wandered off. Police found His Scruffiness, and told him to stay away.

**11:16 a.m.** A woman reported that while out to dinner with her husband the previous evening, she drank about two-thirds of a margarita and began feeling odd – paranoid. She asked her husband if she was chewing her food right and if others could see her eating. She wasn't even sure if she could walk out; he might have to carry her. She made it home OK that night.

**12:13 p.m.** Another scruffy one, wandering in and out of

traffic and yelling on Samoa Boulevard.

**12:33 p.m.** A medical marijuana patient sparked up a bowl in Redwood Park.

**7:39 p.m.** There it is again – the term "scruffy," redolent with the husky scent and free-range coiffure of a wandering cur, applied to a man who ever-so-loudly refused to leave a 13th Street marketplace. "I was standing in the checkout line, and suddenly, from the produce section, erupted yelling and obscenities," said a witness. "He was really raving – I mean, there was spittle flying onto the produce workers." When asked to leave, the scruffster bellowed that "You're violating my civil rights! I'm going down to the Peace and Justice Center!" With that, mutt-man took a noisy trot down H Street toward the Plaza, barking more obscenities, and growling that Arcata is a "racist town." He was described as balding, with a beard and backpack. And *scruffy*.

**9:26 p.m.**
Honey, let's rent us a room
Where our ongoing fight can resume
You scream while I yell
Cops arrive, what the hell?
Behold the high-maint bride and groom.

• **Saturday, May 25 12:19 p.m.** The arboreal cathedral of Redwood Park's towering tree canopy is best experienced with one's brain awash in pleasurechems, or so goes one train of so-called thought.

**3:35 p.m.** THC-induced paranoia is entirely appropriate in the Redwood Park 14th Street nugmart these days, as watchful eyes gaze down from the forested hills, just waiting for buds and bucks to change hands. And when they do...

• **Sunday, May 26 12:44 p.m.** It probably wasn't a Mensa

fundraiser, that yard sale advertised by placards placed directly over traffic signs at Janes Road and Spear Avenue. An officer uncovered the road signs and had a talk with the yard sale's marketing department.

• **Tuesday, May 28 1:33 p.m.** It's not that Ranger Bob is Dick Tracy; more that the cannabis-befuddled stoners-by in Redwood Park's 14th Street lot barely realize a cop's standing there before they're trying to remember how to spell their name when they sign the ticket. One alleged fried-egg-in-a-skillet brain was jailed on charges of possession for sale of marijuana.

**5:22 p.m.** A 12-year-old zoomed around 11th and Larry streets on a motorized three-wheeled vehicle with no license or helmet. Parents were no-no-tified.

**5:23 p.m.** A man ripped off his brother's tools and sold them to buy drugs.

**7:54 p.m.** A man threw an egg at a parked truck on upper H Street and barely had time to savor the conquest when a woman who'd seen the attack ran out and yelled at him. At this he ran off westward, with naught but rivulets of splattered albumen left the tale to tell.

• **Wednesday, May 29 7:17 a.m.** An I Street cooperative supermarket barely got underway for the day when employees had to deal with the first alleged ripoff attempt.

**12:36 p.m.** At least the 13th Street marketplace made it to the noon hour before shopliftingness' first finale.

**2:47–4:01 p.m.** Dirty deeds done dirt cheap in Redwood Park.

**5:11 p.m.** A boy-girl bout of fisticuffs outside an historic Plaza storehouse had an explanation about as easily understood as love. She said they'd been arguing when he made a motion that suggested a blow was coming, and a male bystander confirmed this. Another guy said the guy she'd been arguing with had assaulted her, and he'd tracked him down for an argument during which, both admitted, they'd spat on each other. She said the threatening gesture guy had told her he was going to show up at her house later and "finish things." After some talk about restraining orders, everyone headed out in separate directions.

**8:45 p.m.** There's no recorded instance of trailer park tensions actually being solved to everyone's satisfaction with the use of *nunchuk* sticks, yet a young man was seen brandishing the martial arts weapon and a well-tended mullet hairdo at neighbors and had even exacted punishment on a car. A purposeful cocktail bolstering had preceded the display.

• **Thursday, May 30 2:08 a.m.** For the second time in recent memory, a piece of furniture was discovered aflame in Adams Court. The prior incident involved a chair – obviously a "gateway" furnishing leading to larger sacrificial sitting devices – and this night a burning couch. Next time, it could be the hard stuff – an end table. As is customary, three half-seen males skulked away into the shadows.

**More found notes, from a crime victim/avenger and a hungry/frustrated lunch seeker.**

**2:19 a.m.** *Ha ha,* traffic cones placed at random in the street. What will they think of next, and can they do so sometime soon?

**2:33 a.m.** An unholy agglomeration of sonic stylings, including plangent elements of Varese and Zappa punctuated by early *Terminator* battlebot bombast and tinged with pre-Armageddon junkyard clamor arose from a Stewart Court home. A creative raccoon scampered away in the officer's flashlight beam.

**3:31 a.m.** A man got in some quality staggering-in-and-out-of-traffic time on 17th Street.

**5:50 a.m.** Perhaps in training for his future as an Arcata staggerer, a male person was seen stumbling near Seventh and H streets.

**3:21 p.m.** A man giving away puppies at an F Street supermarket had a novel motivational spiel – any which aren't adopted will be thrown from a bridge, he said. The pups were instead taken to the Humane Society.

**• Friday, May 31 1:28 a.m.** Tensions ran high in a Plaza tavern. Or maybe it was a form of therapy, that one guy reportedly trying to fight someone about some old business from a year ago. Mr. Profiles in Resentment had to suck it up and move on.

**10:54 a.m.** The person who had the bright idea of involving their poochie in a barbecue had to escort the aroma-crazed pet home.

**Noon**
Travelers, fighting
Neither chose to press charges
But that warrant – *ouch!*

**5:34 p.m.**
A hang-up phone call
Star 69 rang a person
Restraining ordered.

**9:55 p.m.** Drawn to Q Street on a report of people fighting, police cited a suspect for carrying alcohol in a vehicle while underage, garnished with marijuana.

• **Saturday, June 1 2:05 a.m.** *Look ma, no brains* – driving the wrong way along Tavern Row right after the bars close!

**2:16 p.m.** A man who thought the honor system would protect his valuables in an unlocked car learned that ethical constraints in parking lots generally bear on whether anyone's looking or not. In this case, no one was.

**2:51 p.m.** A guy wore a blue towel, and that was all, to the Library. Employees said they weren't concerned.

• **Monday, June 6:07 p.m.** A man acting under cocktail-o-matic immunity stood in the middle of South I Street and stopped a woman's car in order to speak strangely to her. Another shackled-drunk shuffle on Samoa Boulevard.

**7:52 p.m.** Images of a firearm pointed at a child broke the routine of a photo development technician at an F Street variety store. Police decided the shots were of a pellet gun, with another child pretending to be frightened.

**8:50 p.m.** A loose dog roved Cedar Avenue, even running up on a woman's porch, much to her exasperation. The dog's owner unconvincingly claimed it had been chained, but was warned anyway. When police left, the woman endured the dog owner's mocking taunts of *"Here, kitty, kitty, kitty,"* which she interpreted as a call to her cat to lure it into the doggie danger zone.

**11:11 p.m.** We may assume the somewhat flattened ex-opossum at Seventh and K streets would've sucked at Frogger.

• **Tuesday, June 4 9:36 a.m.** Is it elitist to not want to look at a stranger lolling around behind your house drinking from a bag at 9:36 a.m.?

**12:01 p.m.** Foul cigarette stink envelopes those who enter an I Street cooperative supermarket, especially when this guy is hanging around. An officer stood by while the odor-adder was ordered elsewhere.

**12:51 p.m.** *Minimalist verse from an APD dispatcher regarding a call for service in the 1500 block of 12th Street:*
Pick up dog
Dog picked up.

**6:32 p.m.** A southside neighbor of Stewart Park reported the "Humboldt Fun Club" ruining the park's grass – they apparently not aware of the park's status as a grass museum with its main exhibit off limits to anyone attempting to have actual fun. The neighbor said he was "taking pictures to identify drug dealers" amongst the funsters. An officer met with the concerned citizen and encouraged him to call police if he witnesses any violations.

**10:32 p.m.** A fist-flavored brouhaha involving 10 combatants outside a 10th Street brewery.

**• Wednesday, June 5 3:08 a.m.** *Oops* – one of life's little *faux pas* has to do with an errant body part tapping the car horn while one is ripping the car stereo out of a dashboard in a vehicle on Chester Avenue. The clumsy thief made good his escape.

**10:34 a.m.** Attempting perhaps to forge some kind of gender equity in terms of the number of semi-feral malcontents with special needs roaming Arcata's streets, a female hitchhiker yelled obscenities at passing cars at Samoa Boulevard and Union Street.

**4:32 p.m.** Living life to its fullest, a resident of South H Street chased people with a stick while serenading them with an obscene tirade. Police called it disturbing the peace, and arrested him.

**• Thursday, June 6 12:22 p.m.** A big, strong Stewart Park neighbor reportedly told schoolchildren they couldn't use the neighborhood park, while in fact, they can, did and will continue to. So who made him the Jell-O Sheriff?

**7:38 p.m.** The place: an I Street cooperative supermarket. A thief's quarry: a can of beer. A foot chase ensued.

**8:02 p.m.** For reasons unfathomable, someone became inordinately vehement at the Valley West Dollar Tree store. Perhaps it was confusion over pricing.

**• Sunday, June 9 12:41-54 a.m.** A male specimen was deemed too pickled to populate a Plaza tavern, where drama nonetheless escalated with the breaking of a pool cue. The stick snapper agreed to pay for the damage.

**10:23 p.m.** A loose dog trotted into a budget motel room in Valley West, and when the lodger went to pet it, the dog clamped its jaws on his right index finger. The dog was secured in a motel room and the owner contacted. She said she didn't have the records to prove it, but the dog had been vaccinated. The toothsome pooch was taken to the micro-pound at the Corp Yard for observation.

**• Monday, June 10 10:06 a.m.** A "desperate" looking man panhandled a dog grooming business in Sunny Brae, making a dog nervous. It began barking, and he fled.

**1:25 p.m.** Most people really don't need their lingering sense of malaise augmented these days, but a woman reported some guy writing down her license plate number while her car was parked out front of her house.

**1:55 p.m.**
Two panhandlers stood at a store
And passersby heard them implore
For cash handouts? Nope.
This pair pined for dope
But never did manage to score.

**2:49 p.m.** A man stood inside one of the free-standing storage units at Ninth and L streets, screaming. He told an officer he was just having a bad day, and was venting in the roadside echo chamber.

**4:10 p.m.** A puppy was untied from a fence in the 900 block of H Street and taken to the City pound. Eventually a wandering waif turned up asking for the pup. She was given back her backpack and bag of dog food, but would have to retrieve the life form the next day. She wasn't very friendly with Babylon's overlords.

**• Tuesday, June 11 10:28 a.m.** A southside Stewart Park neighbor reported two large groups of children numbering about 50 using the park, "There is nothing you can do until you figure this out," he reportedly said. The vigilant neighbor claimed that organized groups – in this case, kids celebrating the end of their elementary school year – are required to obtain permits. He said he'd be taking "covert pictures" of the children out of his bathroom window.

**11:04 a.m.** Some dudes chugged from a bong at the Intermodal Transient Facility.

**12:19 p.m.** To some, the sight and sound of little children playing and laughing is a delight. But to Grinch-like recluses, the idea of anyone having carefree fun in the sunshine is a matter for police intervention. An officer observed groups of schoolkids eating their lunch in Stewart Park making those awful children noises, and their teacher said she'd clean up any leftover litter.

**2:51 p.m.** Every so often a traveler sort of adopts an historic Plaza storehouse as his base of operations, enjoying the amenities and, living life to its fullest, enveloping all who enter and leave in billowing cigarette smoke. A beard-and-backpack equipped miasmatician was motivated to motate.

**9:04 p.m.** He's a fast-walkin', girl-followin', house-starin'-

at, hangin'-out-in-the-area-for-three-hours kinda traveler with beverage breath and his own way of car-campin' at Arcata's westernmost retail business. She's a cop-callin', freak-describin' innocent passerby lookin' out for her neighborhood and fightin' crime. Together, they take up space in the coplog. Catch the action here every Tuesday in the *Arcata Eye*.

**10:10 p.m.** Two large dogs swaggered up and down Heather Lane, flashing their jaws here and there and having a good old time. The pair pranced back home with big dog smiles before the cops came.

**• Wednesday, June 12 10:16 a.m.** Surveying the ruins of the trailer, destroyed by his girlfriend just 10 minutes, earlier, there was little left for the Olympia Street resident to do but phone police.

**4:22 p.m.** A suspect was arrested in Redwood Park on charges of possession of somewhat non-standard naturalist implements – marijuana and a hypodermic syringe.

**9:37–11:46 p.m.** Repeated cocktail inoculations qualified several men for an overnight vacation in the exotic wilds of the Pink House.

**• Thursday, June 13 2:55 a.m.** A graffitist smeared a swath of brown pictograms across three businesses from Uniontown to the Plaza.

**3:23 a.m.** More graffiti moron prints at the high school, plus some locks glued.

**10:38 p.m.** Two representatives of the non-cost effective gender were seen on a license-plateless motorcycle in a school parking lot, shaking paint cans. Then they zoomed.

• **Friday, June 14 12:58 a.m.** The whereabouts of Jeanne Kirkpatrick, Stephen Hawking and Alexander Solzhenitsin at the time are unknown, but *somebody* slathered a Sunny Brae school with soda, toilet paper, ketchup and syrup.

**10:55–11:55 p.m.** Drunks came to a steely end.

• **Monday, June 17 5:16 p.m.**
Near Wyatt Lane, cows took some knocks
From mouth-breathers playing with rocks
They pelted the cattle
Then broke off the battle
And dragged knuckles on down the block.

• **Tuesday, June 18 1:33 p.m.**
Up by Redwood Park
Wayward missiles bore pigment
*Splat!* went the paintball.

• **Wednesday, June 19 2:52 p.m.** An enterprising chap wearing a sandwich board peddled "goods" near an I Street information kiosk. Business license? *Moi?*

**3:25 p.m.** A doggie in bondage at a Union Street high-density residential inn was taken to pooch prison, and a note left in its water dish explaining matters to the human.

**7:08 p.m.** The wife sought succor in her car in the driveway while her husband threw objects around inside their trailer. Police stood by while she retrieved her belongings.

**7:40 p.m.** A residential minivan parked on the Plaza discharged a vile foamy liquid into the gutter. It looked like dishwater to an officer.

**11:08 p.m.** A windshield-buster had a smashing good time on Union Street, and a suspect was arrested.

**11:39 p.m.** An apartment dweller told a neighbor he was "going psycho," and may have done so, since there was no response to an officer's knock at the door.

• **Thursday, June 20 1:31 p.m.** Barking is contagious, at least on Heather Lane – first loose dogs do it, then neighbors chime in, directing arfs at each other.

**8:26 p.m.** Rampant barbarity in Stewart Park again raised its exaggerated head, with a report that someone was tearing the bars from the windows on the south side. Actually, a traveler was trying to use the bars as an opener for a can of food. After logging another in an endless succession of minor annoyances, time-consuming logistical setbacks and admonitions by authority figures, he decided that it would be best if he left.

- **Friday, June 21 11:31 a.m.**
A car battery
Tossed at 11th and H
HazMat training pays.

- **Saturday, June 22 9:42 a.m.** A large blonde dog's sniffer led it inexorably to an I Street Mexican bagel shop, where it was taken into custody.

**10:59 a.m.** A practitioner of the art of dumpster crouching on Giuntoli Lane completed his furtive mission before police arrived.

- **Sunday, June 23 12:24 a.m.** A small squad of male performance artists or idiots smashed bottles in the roadway at Alliance Road and Stromberg Avenue. Police cleared the larger chunks; no sign of the lunks.

**1:01 a.m.** Time to don the old baseball cap and zoom around on a motorized skateboard behind the 24-hour supermarket.

**1:24 a.m.** There was no "Free Stuff" sign on the items left in a car in the 1000 block of H Street, but that didn't stop someone from taking the large tan straw purse with leather straps along with a wool blanket distinguished by blue, green and black geometric patterns and a bird emblem in the middle.

**2:18 a.m.** Some kind of to-do involving Guitar Dan led police on a foot patrol from the newly decommissioned Fun Bunch World Headquarters along the train tracks to the southeast side of the Old Creamery.

**10:23 a.m.** A bike lock that might be fine for Tyee City, Finntown or Crannell could never withstand college town-adapted predators, such as those who rove Foster Avenue.

**11:40 a.m.** Parents tried to dress a fussing child on upper H Street, found their own inner child and took to fussing themselves.

**3:24 p.m.**
The park ranger/doper ballet
Played out in the usual way
With Bob harshing mellows
Of Redwood Park fellows
Who went to Big Pink for the day.

**Just another day on the Plaza.**

**4 p.m.** A malicious mischief call began in the trailer park, where a dad 'n' lad gave voice to their differences – something about a gun was overheard. Next, a beer bottle sailed out into the street – never a good sign – and someone was said to be bleeding from the head. One of the antagonists was tracked down in the gravel quarry parking lot. They'll all laugh about it someday.

**5:40 p.m.** A motor scooterist's good fortune on discovering well-groomed, uncrowded trails on which to buzz about in Redwood Park soon learned the reason for the trails' unspoiled nature – his kind ain't allowed there.

**6:25 p.m.** Unspecified stuff was located along a Redwood Park trail by an "honest transient," who turned it in.

**7:53 p.m.** A traveler who had been "grazing" the yummies on display at a 13th Street marketplace was arrested on a shoplifting charge.

**• Wednesday, June 26 3:12 a.m.** An officer passing a near-Northtown restaurant noticed the owner in the front lobby swigging a beer with Guitar Dan. The restaurateur was advised he couldn't drink in the biz after hours, which he didn't know. The beers were poured out and the state Alcoholic Beverage Control notified. Dan went on to his next wacky misadventure.

**3:14 a.m.** Someone relocated park benches from Stewart Park to the driveway of certain southside residents and placed eggs and concrete atop them.

**3:18 p.m.**
A gaggle of travelers, two and four-footed
Emerged from an area heavily wooded
Where, it is thought, they had fashioned a camp
Down Bayside Road headed toward Union they tramped
But coply response there was somewhat delayed
And they never caught sight of the fuzzy parade.

**• Thursday, June 27 12:56 a.m.** A man gave a ride to two traveling strangers, who rewarded him by taking his wallet and running away near the Plaza. One suspect had a beard and a reddish dog.

**3:29 p.m.** "I haven't forgot about you," said the phone message from an employee who'd been fired a year ago.

• **Friday, June 28 12:17 a.m.** Self-administered cocktail therapy led a man to meditate on the circuit breaker box to a downtown business, where he took understandable delight in flipping the power switches off. Exasperated employees detained him, and police logged another public drunkenness arrest.

**6:41 a.m.** Big bonus bags o' pot trimmings and household garbage appeared in a Westwood Center supermarket's dumpster. Padlock time.

**9:50 a.m.** A little silver car drove up to the 14th Street side of Redwood Park, where a man got out, waved an axe around and declared, "Don't mind me, I'm crazy." The master of the obvious then hopped back in the little car and drove away.

**1:05 p.m.** A quartet of travelers enjoying the redwood rainforest through a bluish miasma of dope smoke were informed as to the error of their alleged ways in Redwood Park.

**4:26 p.m.**
Safe from Ranger Bob
In this cranny of the... *Awww!*
*How'd you find us here?*

**5:15 p.m.** Witnesses said a Plazagoer wore a yellow shirt and gray pants. That is, up until he took off his pants and started cleansing his genital package in the drinking fountain. A policeman was summoned, and no one who'd observed the jarring scene wanted to bestir their memories by subjecting themselves to formal complaint rigmarole. And no one was very thirsty either.

**4:15 p.m.** "Here's some money. Go pick up my prescription, thanks." But neither medicine nor money ever returned.

**9:17 p.m.** A space/time wormhole opened up near the storage units by the freeway, disgorging three "hippies," their ample tresses defying gender identification. An officer conferred with the flower children, who like, kept on going on.

• **Monday, July 1 11:35 a.m.** The remnants of the once-proud Fun Bunch were shooed away from their train track lair by an officer who again mentioned the letter from the defunct railroad which says the disused tracks ought to rust in peace.

# IMBROGLIO EXTRA

## ROCKIN' GLOSSARY

OF **POLICE LOG** TERMS

*An Historic Plaza Storehouse* – There's only one.

*Big Bill* – See McKinley.

*Bongos* – Percussion instrument of Cuban origin, frequently employed as trance-inducing/torture device on the Arcata Plaza.

*Bonking* – Bongo flagellation. Means something else in England.

*Breakfast Club* – They who drink from bags in a secluded Marsh hollow.

*Bro* – Short for "brother," often ineffectually utilized for mercenary endearment purposes by panhandlers.

*Coplog* – Shorthand for the Police Log.

*Dine 'n' dash* – See Scarf 'n' scram.

*Dirt Merchant Central* – See Ninth and H.

*Djmbe, conga* – Along with other hand drums, often mistaken for bongos.

*Dude*– See Man.

*Fill 'n' flee* – To engorge your 12 mpg Planet Killer with dead dinosaurs from places where they hate us, then roar away without remunerating the underpaid attendant.

*420* – A number associated with cannabis self-obfuscation.

*Fun Bunch* – Travelers who meet in the railroad easement behind a mini-storage yard.

*Fun Bunch World Headquarters* – Trackside lair of the Fun Bunch.

*Gauntlet, The* – See Ninth and H.

*Guitar Dan* – Dan Stephens, official minstrel of the Fun Bunch and Breakfast Club.

*Heroin Heights* – A working class neighborhood south of Samoa Boulevard.

*Hovel grovelers* – See Scrounge lizards.

*Intermodal Transient Facility* – The Intermodal Transit Facility, an award-winning dysfunctional building created in 1994, located across from the Arcata Service Center.

*I Street Cooperative Supermarket* – The Arcata Co-op, store of legend and aisleway huggery.

*Judo Hut* – See Udo Ut.

*Man* – Often pronounced *"Myaan"* and utilized as a term of ingratiation. See Bro.

*Marsh* – The Arcata Marsh and Wildlife Sanctuary.

*McKinley* – Twenty-fifth U.S. president, immortalized in a statue on Arcata's town square.

*Mojo-harshing* – Brutal oppression exercised by law enforcement having to do with interrupting cosmic bongo vibes.

*Ninth and H streets* – Also known as The Gauntlet, a street-corner when sitarounders, hangabouts, dirt merchants, nomads and police congregate. Newly regentrified for your convenience as of 2003.

*Nugs* – Cannabis gemlets traded 'twixt Plazoids and beyond.

*The Plaza* – Arcata's multidimensional town square, home to statue of William McKinley.

*Pink House* – The Humboldt County Correctional Facility.

*Pirate, The* – L. Scott Rebman, deceased.

*Ragman* – Pete Villarreal, aka Rags, aka Raggedy Pete.

*Ranger Bob* – Bob Murphy, Arcata Park Ranger.

*Redwood Park* – A great meadow surrounded by redwood trees. The City of Arcata's premier park.

*Scarf 'n' scram* – To eat a restaurant meal and bail on the bill. See dine 'n' dash.

*Schwazz* – The Plaza in stoner.

*Scrounge lizards* – Ninth and H habituees.

*Scroungeloids* – See Scrounge lizards.

*Spanging* – Spare changing.

*Tavern Row* – The line of bars along the Plaza's north side. Also called Bar Row.

*Thirteenth Street marketplace, A* – Wildberries Marketplace, your supermarket of choice.

*Udo Ut* – The Judo Hut, a multi-use City of Arcata building where the J and H on the sign have freakishly withered away.

# IMBROGLIO EXTRA

## SCANDALOUS
# HEADLINES

FROM THE POLICE LOG

Snitty lashout soothes loss of wagon wheel
Fashions of the fussy and fuzzy
Drizzle-drenched dumpster stirs passions
Parking spot hegemonists lean in retaliation
Green flower savior takes hose in hand
Kissy-face scenario eludes smitten swain
Bearded man - yeah, him - wanders aimlessly
Porch, playground provide drunkard habitat
Interrupted while shopping at the free money
store
Crazy-large ladies, nasty notes and wall
waterers
Someone should make a book of this crap
Wanted woman throttles log with garden hose
Barbarous hordes peril landscaping
Donut dispensary hosts unholy drama
Brainiac biker bus-bumped, bummed
Bongos, beggars braise consciousness
He needed somewhat more pants than that
Trees are for stabbing
Tailgated senior goes digital
He said, she said, while others arfed
Arcata umbrage farm yields harvest of
resentment
Rolling bongo thunder becomes petite pitter
patter

Rapid  response requires rigid digit
deployment
Flung  foliage tempers anguish over hippie
proliferation
Unrequited  lust leaves suitor cash and germ-
free
Well,  that certainly got everyone's attention
Venting's  various versions
That'll put a dent in your day
Arcata – the vast wasteland
It lives in the walls and moves by night
Roving,  raving redhead reaps words' worth
Street  musicians pioneer new sub-genre
Bongos,  bagpipes put out of your misery
Free-lance  fungibility fizzles
Keep  your meat out of the street
Gravity  proves a canny, cunning adversary
Scroungeloid  scalvagers shown error of
slobly ways
Lotion  conscripted to evil purpose;
ice cream cleared of wrongdoing
The  Dimwit Days Migratory Birdbrain Festival
White  T-shirt dreamboat maroons date by
dumpsters
Motive,  means and opportunity (and mustard)
Laundry  room campout dissolves in swirl of
pills
Mischievous  mind games manifest in desultory
devilment
What's  with all the wee-wee?
If  you can't steal it, wreck it
Parking  spot hegemonists lean in retaliation
Drizzle-drenched  dumpster stirs passions
Fashions  of the fussy and fuzzy

# Subscribe to the Arcata Eye.

## It's a real weekly newspaper!

Details at www.arcataeye/com/about

# ᴵNim–räd
**1.** A person regarded as silly, foolish or stupid.
*Example* A wee-hour bongo stylist.

# Im–ᴵbrOl–(ᴵᴵ)yO
**1.** An intricate or perplexing situation (as in a drama or novel), misunderstanding, disagreement, etc., of a complicated or bitter nature, as between persons or nations.
**2.** A violently confused or bitterly complicated altercation.
**3.** A confused heap.